PACIFIC VOYAGE

A YEAR ON THE ESCORT CARRIER
HMS ARBITER DURING WWII

To/ John

with best wishes

Peter Ward

15.1.2014

PACIFIC VOYAGE

A YEAR ON THE ESCORT CARRIER
HMS ARBITER DURING WWII

Peter Ward

BREWIN BOOKS

First published by
Brewin Books Ltd, 56 Alcester Road,
Studley, Warwickshire B80 7LG in 2005
www.brewinbooks.com

ISBN 1 85858 276 8

A Cataloguing in Publication Record
for this title is available from the British Library.

Typeset in Stempel Garamond
Printed in Great Britain by
The Cromwell Press

CONTENTS

*(The places visited during the 60,000 miles trip
are described as they were at the time)*

ILLUSTRATIONS

FOREWORD

I was fortunate to find the publisher Brewin Books for my first book, 'From Africa to the Arctic' (A year on the destroyer HMS Beagle during World War II), launched by Ottakars Bookshop in April 2003. Unlike the present book 'A Pacific Journey' (A year on HMS Arbiter – Escort Carrier), I had kept a daily diary for the 'Beagle' year, giving me a head start – there is no diary for the 'Arbiter'. Nevertheless the P.R.O. at Kew Gardens hold Log Books for each of the months that I served in the Far East ('Beagle's' Log Books are lost!), and it was with some relief that I was able to unearth a quantity of invaluable memorabilia, including a newspaper published in the area of our operation at the time, together with many photographs – we had a official photographer aboard the 'Arbiter'. One of the crew members had produced a map recording our 60,000 miles round trip with, most importantly, the dates of our visits to the places en route, an invaluable skeleton on which to build.

It was with some trepidation that I started 'A Pacific Journey' (without a diary), but memory, memorabilia and pictures soon established a basis for further research and determination. I use the word 'determination' advisably, there being much less written about the war with Japan and the British Pacific Fleet's contribution than has been available about other theatres of war (especially the hostilities in Europe) an opinion stressed by the writer Peter C. Smith in his book 'Task Force 57'. His book is a thorough record of the Pacific War, the events leading up to BPF, its contribution to Japan's surrender, and the aftermath.

I consider myself relatively lucky to have survived patrolling the North Atlantic Ice Barrier in a Corvette, HMS Sweet Briar, in search of a German Battleship! – sitting on Sunk Head Sands off the East Coast, in a concrete Fort, for a year – battling with the elements, the environment and the enemy off the coast of West Africa and during convoys to and fro Murmansk, etc., Russia, to say nothing of dodging torpedoes – taking part in the 'D' Day Landings on 6th. June and the days that followed. All this, prior to my Far East experience, the burden of this book.

I have written this book, therefore, as another of the few records (albeit brief) of the part that the British Pacific Fleet played in Japan's defeat; a record also of the generosity of the Australian people; a reminder of the sacrifices that were made to ensure the freedom that much of the world enjoys today (at times during the Second World War is was 'touch and go'); and a tribute to all those who took part, those alive to tell the tale and those who paid the ultimate cost.

PREAMBLE

This book, mainly about my experiences as a member of the crew of HMS Arbiter, is only a part of my five years Second World War Royal Naval service and thus I feel a digression to fill in some of the gaps between 4th. October 1941 and 6th. December 1944, when I joined the 'Arbiter', may be of interest.

The word 'Beagle' has many connotations. There is the well-known hunting dog, frequently associated with the fox and controversy, the wooden sailing ship used by Darwin for his expeditions and, more recently, the Beagle 11 exploration of Mars.

For me, the word 'Beagle' means the Second World War and the period of it which is captured in my first book, 'From Africa to the Arctic', a record of my year on the destroyer HMS Beagle, in which I covered the period from June 1943 to June 1944 and described convoys off West Africa, Russian convoys and the 'D' Day Landings. The book was based on a daily Diary and thus the text was determined by recorded events and, with photographs from the Imperial War Museum etc., the main elements therefore, were proscribed. The detail of my year aboard HMS Beagle (the Royal Naval destroyer I hasten to add!) can be found elsewhere, as mentioned earlier.

This book, concerning a year on the Aircraft Carrier, HMS Arbiter, is a different ball game, there being no diary but a great number of photographs of my own, many taken by a tame photographer, a member of the crew. In my book about the Beagle I touch upon life before and after that experience, and I feel that before recounting my life on the 'Arbiter', a little more detail about these other commitments during my five years in the war-time Royal Navy is appropriate.

I joined the Royal Navy as an Ordinary Seaman at HMS Glendower (once a Butlin's Holiday Camp, but no longer!) Pwllheli, North Wales. Our training consisted mainly of improving our fitness, one of the things I was to regret for many years? During the physical fitness training, one of the activities involved the group in forming four lines, each individual instructed to link to the man in front by putting our hands on his shoulders. We then proceeded to 'follow the leader', keeping in lines (a rather unusual activity for 'War' training?). Unfortunately the tail of our line swung out, bringing the last man's shoulder into contact with the next line – I was the last man!!! And the result was a dislocated shoulder. Fortunately the shoulder joint regained normality fairly quickly. Nevertheless, I informed the physical training instructor, who looked at me rather quizzically, but had the good sense to send me to the Sick Bay (the medical centre).

The Sick Bay had a reputation for attracting malingerers, so at first I was treated suspiciously (there were always recruits who did their best to avoid duties of any sort) but by now there was enough bruising to substantiate my account of the accident. This meant my coping with my arm in a sling for some time. Now, whether it was the shoulder problem, or the fact that I had volunteered for a Radar course at a centre on the Isle of Man, that caused me to opt out of a boxing match (for which I had volunteered!) I cannot remember, but imagine my relief when I discovered that my opponent was to be a Stoker (engine-room personnel) built like a mountain! Incidentally, the shoulder was to dislocate nine times over the next twenty years or so, twice more during my Naval career.

After six weeks at HMS. Glendower I moved to Douglas, Isle of Man to train as a Radar Operator at the specialist centre on Douglas Head, one of the higher points on the island, and near to our accommodation, the pre war holiday hotels on the sea front.

The hotels were collectively run on the same lines as a Royal Naval vessel. If it had a name, I cannot recall it. The course was very intensive and we had little time to explore the island, that was to come later when the war had ended and when I was a representative at teachers' conference. The three-letter acronym of the union's title pluralized, tended to sum up many of the representatives at that time! I enjoyed my sojourn at Douglas, the elements of the course seemed to suit my aptitudes, but I was in for a rude awakening!

I well remember the situation on the last day of our course. The members of the course were signalled to assemble by the officer in charge. If I remember correctly, we stood in a line in a corridor, to be told that the Radar operator on HMS Sweet Briar had been taken ill and, with the corvette due to depart from Douglas that night, two volunteers from our course were needed to take the sick operator's place. There had been a 'buzz' (rumour) going round that 'Sweet Briar' was going to America but, with hindsight, how credence could have been put on the rumour I cannot imagine. However, naïve Peter Ward volunteered, the only one to do so in our group of about twenty! Another operator had to be 'press ganged', unfortunately, and I do not remember how he was chosen, but it resulted in a married man joining me on our first trip to sea in a vessel of the Royal Navy.

There followed some of the worst days that one could imagine – I lay in a hammock for fully three days, consuming nothing more than bread and water and suffering from violent sea sickness. On regaining some sort of well being, I discovered that we were not heading for America, but for Iceland! Iceland was to be our base for the next four months whilst we carried out patrols to the North Atlantic ice barrier. I ought to mention that the Irish Sea had a reputation for ferocity, each end being open to the Atlantic causing cross currents. I was unlucky in that I encountered one of the rougher seas during those early days on 'Sweet Briar', a real baptism of fire!

Once I had regained some sort of normality, I took on my responsibilities as Radar Operator for some of the time and Bridge Lookout for the rest of my duties. Nothing of moment happened during the trip until we were approaching Iceland. We had left England in darkness (due to the blackout) and it came rather as a shock to see Reykjavik brightly illuminated. Iceland was of course not likely to suffer bombing etc., situated as it was. The sea had been quite rough throughout the trip and we were looking forward to tying up alongside and having a decent night's sleep, more or less impossible at sea as corvettes were like 'corks' in Neptune's playground, when suddenly a great wave hit us on the port bow. These waves, extra large, were referred to as 'green', and 'Sweet Briar' shook from stem to stern. Fortunately we were heading into the waves (intentionally), because had the wave hit us broadside, heaven knows what the outcome would have been. I was Bridge Lookout on the starboard side and was flung across the bridge, managing to hold on to something as the ship righted itself, and heaving a sigh of relief that I and all those on duty on the bridge were all present and correct. Once in harbour and with the ship tied up, hammocks felt like heaven as we all turned in, relieved that the first part of our itinerary had been completed successfully.

Iceland, of course, was covered in snow, very mountainous and very cold, and the hours of daylight were considerably less than those we had experienced in England, Reykjavik being that much farther north. Strangely, I did not feel the cold to the extent that I did back home, and I think that it was because of the dryness of the air. It might have been that my initial training at HMS Glendower had made me that much fitter?

I cannot remember going ashore much, if at all, most of our time being taken up by patrolling the ice barrier considerably north of Iceland, to keep a look-out for a German Pocket Battleship – I think it was the 'Admiral Scheer' – although it might have been the 'Prinz Eugen' a heavy cruiser.

I presume that the thinking behind detailing us for these duties was linked to the supply routes to Russia used by our convoys, warning of the movement of elements of the German Fleet in time to advise the convoy Commodore being of paramount importance. I was under the impression that corvettes, being cheap to carry out these duties in terms of fuel usage, also provided a small target! Having spotted the enemy, we were supposed to make all speed south, all of sixteen knots (!), to rendezvous with a cruiser that would then take over responsibility. This may or may not have been the scenario. One firm memory does stick in my mind and that was a fear that arose and was shared by other members of the crew when the captain decided to plough through the ice floes at a speed of sixteen knots. We could hear sizeable lumps of ice smashing into our hull (we were based in the forward, lower area of the corvette) fashioned from metal plates of no thickness at all (sometimes likened to a sardine tin) expecting penetration at any minute! Fortunately it never occurred, but we could never fathom the wisdom or otherwise of the captain, seemingly speeding for no apparent reason and, to our minds, putting the ship in danger. The captain of course, standing on the bridge, was presumably unaware of the effect the speed through the ice was having on the submerged part of the hull?

Our north Atlantic duty completed, we returned to blighty and, according to my naval record, I spent one night at HMS Pembroke, before making my way to HMS Sunk Head Fort, which sat on the treacherous Sunk Head Sands off the East Coast. I think I was rather miffed at not having some shore leave, but during the war one did as one was bid! The link between the Fort and the mainland was via a trawler, based at Harwich. I well remember the railway journey from London via Manningtree and Colchester.

Sunk Head Fort, situated off Britain's East Coast. Photograph courtesy of the Imperial War Museum, London, A26878.

The Fort consisted of two concrete towers joined to a large concrete base that had been filled with ballast once the Fort had been towed out from the Thames, where it had been constructed. On top of the towers sat a steel deck, on which was mounted a 4.7 inch gun and a Radar cabin. Our job was to protect the shipping lanes off the East Coast. One of the towers, which was without portholes, contained our living quarters and the other was used for stores and equipment. The method adopted for getting to and from the Fort was via a trawler, mentioned earlier. Our kit bags and hammocks were loaded on to a net that had loops on each of the four corners. A derrick lifted the loaded net once the corners had been attached to a hook and swung the contents on to the trawler. Once we reached the Fort, the derrick, with the net still attached, swung the contents aboard the Fort, allowing it to be unloaded.

If my memory serves me correctly, the complement of the Fort was divided into two watches, allowing one watch home leave whilst the other manned the Fort. It is just possible that we spent four weeks on board (the Fort was run as a ship) and two weeks off, but that would have demanded a different organisation.

I joined the 'Fort' on 25th. April 1942 and my tour of duty lasted about a year. Most of the time life was pretty mundane, with normal ship watch duties revealing little of interest, and time off duty taken up by reading, playing cards etc., keeping the mess deck clean and, of course, ourselves.

One incident however sticks out in my mind concerning tobacco. Ship's crews were allowed to take a ration of cigarettes, pipe tobacco etc., ashore on leave, and this was strictly monitored bearing in mind the restrictions suffered by the general populous. We were also allowed a tot of rum each day, with small ships like corvettes, destroyers benefiting from neat rum, as opposed to rum mixed with water (one and one or two and one parts water to rum) which the larger ships had. The particular incident I have in mind concerned neat rum that I had saved (illegally!), you were supposed to drink it at the issuing point, but the boatswain was not always vigilant, and leaf tobacco, an alternative to cigarettes. The trick was to roll the leaf tobacco into a sausage-like shape, called a 'prick' using the neat rum, and binding it to allow it to mature. I had done this not knowing how I was to get it ashore for my father – I did not smoke.

The opportunity was to present itself when, on one of the trips back to the Fort, one of the loops parted from the hook as our belongings were being unloaded. The contents of the net fell into the sea and was taken away by the current. Fortunately the whaler was quickly lowered and those on board managed to pick up most of the things that had dropped. As far as I was concerned it was not a happy occasion, my having taken a violin back with me off leave! The instrument and the case, even in that short time, had been attacked by the salt water and were virtually in pieces – a mixed blessing as it turned out. As I stuck the violin back together again, I stuffed it with the tobacco, using string to hold it together, both violin and case. Leave was due and I walked through the check point trying to look innocent, the military police not suspecting anything! My father was very grateful and I entitled the experience 'my little fiddle'!! I still have a piece of music stained by the North Sea water. In my five years in the Navy I did only one more similar act, but this time I dangled the tobacco down the leg of my trousers. I will leave the rest to your imagination! The fact that the tobacco was not for my own consumption seemed to make it OK at the time. It was a sort of game and I was very young.

The only other memory worthy of note was an attack by two German aircraft, but this lasted only a matter of minutes and the aircraft were scared off by our large gun, oerlikans and small arms. I do not recall with any affection my time on HMS Sunk Head Fort – part of the reason must have been lack of change of scenery (there were no portholes anyway) and ships usually float and go places!

I stayed at various Navy establishments over the next few weeks including HMS Alfred, where I attempted to become an officer, but my face did not fit! Perhaps that would have denied me joining the 'Beagle' that was to be my next assignment, and the publishing of my first book 'From Africa to the Arctic' in April 2003. The book details convoy duties off the West Coast of Africa, Russian Convoys (4 return trips to Murmansk) and the 'D' Day Landings, all based on my Diary (June 1943 to June 1944). See report '60 years on', a visit to Moscow and Murmansk (May, 2005).

After a year on HMS Beagle, I spent several months in a variety of Naval Establishments, including HMS Drake, Heron, Valkyrie, before joining HMS Arbiter, a converted Aircraft Carrier, on 6th. December 1944, the details of which are the basis of my second book, entitled 'Pacific Voyage'.

HMS Beagle.

Dedication: Dedicated to Jean, Nicky and Sue.

'*We must never forget*'.

Chapter One

JOINING HMS ARBITER
AND PREPARING FOR THE PACIFIC

As I said earlier, I joined HMS Arbiter on 4th. December 1944, and from that time until 1st, March 1945 we were involved with preparations for service in the Far East. Our base was Greenock on the River Clyde, an area that I had experienced earlier in the war (on HMS Beagle) and the sight of Ailsa Craig, at the mouth of the river, was not a new phenomenon as we left for exercises, mainly to give pilots practice in taking off and landing on a floating airfield, 'circuits and bumps' as they were called. There were, of course, skills to be honed by the crew as a whole.

It was essential that the pilots, and the personnel on board the Carrier whose duty it was the direct the pilots for safe landings, received as much practice as possible – landing on an aircraft carrier was a tricky manoeuvre. It was the duty of the Captain to maintain a steady course into the wind, balancing the wind speed with the speed of the ship to create an optimum situation for take-off or

Ailsa Craig (near the mouth of the River Clyde) with HMS Verulum.

A Map of HMS Arbiter's 60,000 miles round trip.

landing. The state of the sea was also critical and would sometimes make these activities impossible.

Built in the USA and loaned to Great Britain under 'Lease Lend' at a time when all the stocks in British shipyards were full, she was fitted at Vancouver, British Columbia and was commissioned in March 1944. The commissioning ceremony was preceded by an accident that would have been regarded, if it had happened in olden days, as a 'hoodoo' by superstitious sailors. Whilst a number of ratings were boarding the ship to attend the ceremony, the gangway collapsed and the sailors fell to the floating platform below. Casualties on that occasion were fortunately slight. A less fortunate mishap occurred before the ship was properly under way to take her place as a unit of the Royal Navy; whilst doing trials off Vancouver involving a paravane exercise, two members of her crew were knocked overboard and were drowned.

Despite those setbacks, the 'Arbiter' arrived in the United Kingdom and was immediately utilized for duties in the Atlantic. For several months she did valuable work operating in convoys during a period when the 'Battle of the Atlantic' had again flared up with intensity, following the invasion of Europe. The 'D' Day Landings are also covered in my book 'From Africa to the Arctic'. Not least of this work by HMS Arbiter, was the repatriation to Britain of children who had been evacuated to America and Canada at the beginning of the war, and the ferrying of supplies to maintain the gigantic war machine of the Allies.

After a major refit in Belfast, during which time a number of sailors of her company lost their hearts to some Irish 'colleens', the ship left for the East at the end of February this year. For a time HMS Arbiter operated in the East Indies, but was later transferred to the Pacific where, as a unit of the British Pacific Fleet Train, she did invaluable work. At the end of this period, when preparations were being made for departure to the Far East, the 'Arbiter' received a new Captain. The new commanding officer was Captain D.H. Everett, D.S.O., M.B.E., R.N., who later became Commodore of Hong Kong.

I do not think that I had any idea of the destination of 'Arbiter' when I joined the crew, not that I would have had any choice if I had disapproved! What a stark comparison was engendered when I considered 'Beagle' and 'Arbiter', the

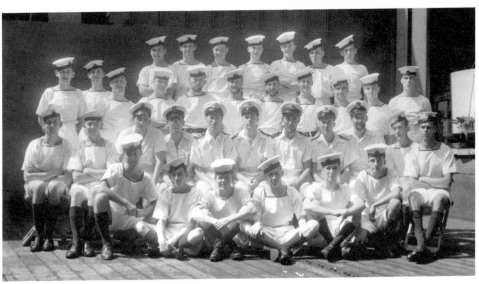

The Radar complement. (Peter Ward seated far left).

former a relatively small destroyer, the latter a rather large aircraft carrier, albeit a converted merchantman.

'Beagle' with its sleek form, seaworthy, well armed and with the bridge forward and central, 'Arbiter' ungainly, top heavy with the added flight deck, poorly armed and with the bridge on the starboard side, well back from the bow, making manoeuvrability difficult and half the speed of the destroyer, HMS Beagle.

I mentioned in my Diary whilst on the 'Beagle' how concerned I was in rough weather when we were rolling rather than pitching because of the possibility of capsizing, remote though it was, well this concern was magnified on the 'Arbiter', especially on the outward journey to the Pacific when the hangar and the flight deck were crammed with aircraft and equipment, making her even less seaworthy. Sometimes she would seem to be about to roll over, the 'angle of lean' being so great, but at the last moment, almost like a great sea monster, she would drag herself upright, only to do the same on the opposite side.

Another comparison worthy of mention concerns personnel and accommodation, the 'Beagle' with its cramped quarters, hammocks and basic cooking facilities and under two hundred members of the crew living cheek by jowl, corresponding with the more spacious mess decks of the 'Arbiter', bunks, a proper canteen with a greater variety of food and, of course, a much larger crew. Obviously the larger the vessel the less the movement created by the sea, or perhaps it would be better to describe the movements as slower and less abrupt.

I mentioned earlier the 'trials' that were necessary to prepare any ship for its proposed contribution to the war effort, and this meant practising certain skills and manoeuvres over and over again until they became second nature. Not only did this give the pilots and those responsible for safe landings plenty of practice, but it enabled the Radar equipment to be calibrated to ensure correct distances etc., were shown on the Radar screens, gave us operators plenty of experience and established proper communication procedures with the 'plot', the operational nerve centre of the ship. In the event of 'Arbiter' being involved in action, everything had to work like clockwork.

Leave was granted from time to time and this allowed us to travel home to see our families and, of course, shore leave enabled us to see something of Scotland around the Greenock area, not particularly exciting!

When it was deemed that 'Arbiter' was ready to meet the requirements of the Pacific War, the carrier was crammed full of aircraft and equipment, both in the very large hangar and on deck - there was hardly any room to move. I think that the aircraft were Corsairs, their wings folded upwards thus saving space.

An example of refuelling at sea during 'Trials'.

But before there was any thought of 'Arbiter' leaving for the Far East, there were to be three months of intense activity that included a major refit in the Belfast shipyards, training and trials in the waters between Ireland and Scotland, Greenock being our last port of call before the departure for our Pacific Voyage.

One usually thinks of 'circuits and bumps' in terms of aircraft practising taking off and landing on terra firmer, but it can also include the same procedures for aircraft carrier pilots. Needless to say the situation for Royal Navy pilots is considerable more hazardous, the landing surface being unpredictable. In my first book 'From Africa to the Arctic' I describe a tragic situation whilst HMS Beagle was on Russian Convoy escort duty, when an aircraft attempted to land on the flight deck of HMS Tracker during particularly rough weather and missed the deck, crashing into the gun on the deck below, with fatal consequences, having misjudged the rise and fall of the carrier.

During trials before setting out on the long voyage to Australia, when pilots due for service in the fight against Japan practised the afore mentioned techniques of taking off and landing, HMS Arbiter being the moving target, members of the

A Corsair landing on the flight deck.

crew, including myself, used to stand on a catwalk on the side of the flight deck, but slightly lower, watching Corsairs take off and land. The take off manoeuvre involved a catapult using steam pressure to assist the aircraft gain enough speed to become airborne and this was mostly successful, only occasionally did an aircraft fail to gain enough momentum, resulting in it crashing into the sea, often a belly-flop, allowing the pilot to escape unharmed, to be picked up by a rescue boat.

Landing on was a very different matter, resulting in more accidents than those involving taking off. As I said earlier, some of us would stand on the catwalk watching the pilots practise these techniques, an activity that proved, on occasion, rather hazardous. The photographs describe one incident better than words, where an aircraft misses the flight deck and careers along the catwalk. You can imagine that we all vanished through to doorways that led on to the catwalk like frightened rabbits. The aircraft settled partly on the flight deck and partly on the catwalk only to fall off the side of 'Arbiter' into the sea upside down, drifting astern and finally, with the tail of the plane visible, vanishing from sight – the pilot was rescued.

Other bizarre incidents included aircraft over-running the landing area of the flight deck and crashing because the hook on the underside rear of the plane failed to contact the slightly raised arrester wires stretched across the flight deck.

A Corsair falling off the catwalk into the sea.

A great deal of responsibility rested with the mechanics that serviced the planes, the flight deck personnel concerned with the organisation required for the take off and the landing of the aircraft, which included the bat-man who guided the aircraft on to the flight deck, indicating to the pilot the need to rise or fall, move right of left, to ensure that he had as much in his favour as possible to negotiate a successful landing.

It is worth mentioning that the aircraft were stored in the hangar below the flight deck and were moved from the hangar to the flight deck via a giant lift which, when fully raised, formed part of the flight deck at the rear of the carrier.

We were at Belfast for practically the whole of January 1945, occupying No.3 Berth, 'C' Dolphin, Musgrave Channel. The order of the day would have been keeping the ship clean, the practising of various skills, with the individual members of the crew attending to their own requirements, dhobeying (washing clothes) etc. Shore leave would have been granted. The Log Book for January gave little other information, detailing certain daily duties and at what times of the day they were carried out.

BELFAST

Capital of Northern Ireland. This great port derived its name from the Gaelic *beol*, a ford, and *farset* or *feirste*, a sandbank. Situated on the River Lagan where it enters Belfast Lough, it was built largely on reclaimed marshland. Although it had few natural advantages, it had risen in a few centuries from an obscure village to the sixth port and eighth city of the U.K. Its ascent to civic greatness dates from the plantation of Ulster in the reign of James 1. For the most part its citizens were of Scottish descent with the traditional characteristics of the Scots.

When Ireland was politically divided in 1920, Belfast became the seat of the Ulster government. The imposing parliament buildings at Stormont and dignified law courts near the city centre were the gift of the U.K. parliament. Other notable

A Map of Belfast at the time of our visit.

buildings were the city hall, built at a cost of £328,879, a good example of Renaissance architecture; the great sandstone Church House, headquarters of the Presbyterian Church in Ireland, which is after the Scottish baronial style; Queen's University, a dignified building in mellow brick; the museum and art gallery; the harbour office, Telephone House and Broadcasting House, headquarters of the Northern Ireland region of the B.B.C. The principal voluntary hospitals were the Royal Victoria, Mater Infirmorum, Children's, Royal Maternity and Ulster Hospital for children and women. At the beginning of the 19th. century the population numbered a bare 25,000; in 1937 it was 438,000.

On the 29th. January 'Arbiter' sailed for Bangor (N.I.) preparing for sea at 0745 and arriving at Bangor at 1315, where we dropped the port anchor. Various exercises were carried out during the trip. The ship was brought up to 5 shackles in 10 fathoms of water. On the 30th. we proceeded to Rothesay Bay, leaving on the next day to sail to 'Tail O'Bank', Greenock via the Clyde exercise area, finally arriving at B5 Berth, where we let go the starboard anchor, bringing the ship up to 4 shackles in 10 fathoms.

According to the Log Book, February was a busy month travelling between Greenock, Largs Bay, Rothesay Bay, Loch Long and Belfast (Airport Wharf, Sydenham), frequently using the Clyde exercise area en route for flying practice and finally arriving back at B5 Berth on 26th. February. Shore leave was granted during this period to fit in with the duty roster.

On the outbreak of the Second Great War, the port of Belfast at once became a naval base and later an Admiralty dockyard. It was mainly from there that operations were carried out against the 'U' Boat menace in the Atlantic. The port was the chief connecting link with the USA after the introduction of Lease Lend, handling vast quantities of foodstuffs and munitions. At its approaches, great convoys assembled for the Atlantic crossing and later for the operations in Europe and the Mediterranean. It was the first landing place for U.S. troops in the British Isles. It is worth remarking that in 1847 the tonnage of vessels cleared from the port was a little over half a million; in 1944 it was nearly five million. Belfast had one of the world's largest graving docks and also a large floating dock, the property of the Admiralty. The port was so extensively used by the Admiralty that sometimes as many as 82 craft were in the harbour at the same time.

The shipbuilding and linen industries were largely responsible for the city's prosperity. Sir Edward Harland, founder of Harland and Wolff, also founded its reputation for turning out great ships. The Queen's Island yards were a hive of industry, output being over one million tons. An aircraft section turned out components for the associated company, Short and Harland, whose main works were also situated at the Queen's Island. Short and Harland's, a subsidiary of Short Bros., Rochester, during the Second World War, produced a large number of aircraft, including 1,500 heavy bombers.

The city suffered severely from air attack during 1941, two being particularly violent (April 15th. and May 4th.) with port installations being badly damaged. The damage to the shipyards was heavier than to any other shipbuilding centre and direct hits were registered on the aircraft plants at Queen's Island.

The harbour was one of the finest in the U.K. It had a quayside of 3,228 lineal feet, and a straight channel to deep water of over 4 miles, giving a waterway with a uniform depth of 32 feet at high water and 23 feet at low. The harbour extended over 2,500 acres, with ten docks and basins of varying capacity. The berthage alongside could take the largest type of aircraft carrier, a facility that was fully exploited, and something that created no problems for a vessel of HMS Arbiter's size.

One memory that stays with me concerning Belfast, bearing in mind the supply of food etc., continually arriving from America, was arriving home on leave after a visit there weighed down with goodies that were severely rationed on the British mainland!

I found myself particularly popular. Being a non-smoker, I was also able to add to the family's delight, especially my father, with some cigarettes.

By 1st. March it was deemed that HMS Arbiter was ready and willing to undertake the duties for which she had been prepared during the last few months, and so we set sail as part of a small convoy to head for Gibraltar, proceeding on a zig zag course (a practise commonly adopted if there was the slightest risk of 'U' Boat activity). Crossing the Bay of Biscay was uneventful, not always the case, as it can be quite rough. We reached the 'Rock' at 1535 on 7th. March and secured the ship alongside, with leave being granted to the Red and White Watches. Although we were berthed at Gibraltar for several days, we were not able to do much exploration, there being the normal disciplines and duties to attend to. Fortunately I was able to return to Gibraltar after the war, whilst holidaying in Morocco with the family.

GIBRALTAR

A town and rock fortress at the southern extremity of Spain, and a British possession. The rock jutted out into the Mediterranean as an attenuated peninsula, ending in Europa Point. The town was divided into two sections – the North Town and the South Town. The North Town was the meaner part of

Gibraltar.

Gibraltar, with narrow and crooked streets. After the war (1947) the upper portion of the fortress was to be turned into a public park. The principal buildings were the Anglican cathedral of the Holy Trinity, built in Moorish style and consecrated in 1832; the church of the Sacred Heart of Jesus; the castle, built by the Moors, and the Governor's residence. Gibraltar was connected with the mainland by an isthmus three miles long and one mile wide.

The mole of Gibraltar Bay afforded secure anchorage for the largest vessels. The town was of great importance as a coaling station. The harbour, of two hundred acres, could accommodate the whole of the Mediterranean Fleet. During the Second World War the fortress of Gibraltar was the base for naval and air operations, controlling shipping through the Straits and along trade routes to South America, West Africa and the Cape. On the loss of the French naval bases, it became the sole Allied Mediterranean base.

Shortly before and during the war the fortifications were strengthened and A.A. batteries were installed. Extensive tunnelling accommodated underground emplacements, hospitals, barracks and stores. The racecourse was converted into an aerodrome. In July, some 15,000 women and children were taken off, the majority going to England. The people began to return in 1944. Population estimated at 19,232.

THE MEDITERRANEAN

Our trip from Gibraltar to Port Said was somewhat uneventful, 'Arbiter' ploughing a lone furrow through this virtually inland sea that, like the Irish Sea, could be as docile as a lamb or diabolically rough. Fortunately we experienced the former. I think we tended to follow the North African coastline and were considered not important enough to warrant attention, in spite of our valuable cargo of aircraft and supplies. Earlier in the war, the Mediterranean had experienced a very different scenario. It was just as well that the weather looked kindly upon us, bearing in mind that the flight deck was filled, cheek by jowl, with aircraft etc., as was the hangar. Had the weather been difficult, as it was on our return journey, and the planes and other cargo had started to move, the outcome could have been disastrous. I think that it was with some relief that we tied up at Port Said.

PORT SAID

A town in Egypt at the north entrance to the Suez Canal. It stood on land reclaimed from the sea, and was founded in 1859, when the first surveys for the canal were made. Offices established there included the Suez Canal Co., and various mercantile and steamship companies. Port Said was named after Said Pasha, the promoter of the canal, and was of great importance as a coaling station and shipping centre for Suez traffic. Population approximately 124,749.

Port Said: 1. Suez Canal Company's Office. 2. Lessop's statue as seen from the breakwater. 3. A general view. 4. Houses in the native quarter.

Chapter Two

JOURNEY TO INDIA

As I said earlier, we left the Clyde, in convoy, on 1st. March, and were at sea until 7th. when we reached Gibraltar. During this sea trip (March 2nd. 3rd. 4th. 5th. 6th.) we adopted a zig zag course (in case the odd 'U' Boat was still lurking) and mounted dawn and dusk 'action stations', the times when ships are most vulnerable, and to keep members of the crew on their toes and ready for any eventuality. We spent 4 days at Gibraltar, leaving at 0740 on the 11th. engaging in a flying programme, duly completed by 1635. Pilots and support crews needed as much practice as possible to successfully negotiate the complications involved is taking off and landing on a flight deck. Nothing of particular interest occurred during our 'cruise' through the Mediterranean Sea, although the Log Book does mention a torpedo exercise in which 'Arbiter' was engaged, with the help of the destroyer HMS Verulum, from 1908 to 2000. Our speed, incidentally, was 18 knots – probably our top speed, but the speed of ships during the war was important in calculating fuel consumption.

Port Said was reached on 18th. March, and the ship was secured using E Berth, Port Said Harbour at 1400, leave being granted. At 1730 we took on 361 tons of fuel oil and 18 tons of diesel. Leaving Port Said at 0618 on 19th. March, we took on two pilots from the Suez Canal Company, every ship passing through the canal having to meet this demand, the reason being that the pilots were experienced in negotiating this stretch of water. In my description of the canal, I emphasise the changing nature of the canal, sometimes very narrow, contrasting with large expanses of water in the form of lakes. A large amount of shipping passed through this 'lifeline' to the Far East etc., and an accident causing a blockage would have been catastrophic. The two pages of the Log Book Records fill in the detail of arrival at Port Suez and the canal trip to Port Suez. Our stay at Port Suez was short, and on the 20th. March we headed for Bombay, reaching there on the 28th. dropping anchor at 1400. Leave was granted. Elsewhere the reader can peruse a description of Bombay, although our stay again was rather short – we left there at 2015 on the 29th. March, adopting zig zag No.12 at 2345. Our next port of call was to be Ceylon.

18th. March 1945 – Log Book Record (Gibraltar to Port Said).

Ante Meridian.

0038	A/Co. (Altered Course) 100 degrees, speed 15 knots.
0112	A/Co. 050 Deg.
0235	Rosetta St. bearing 085 deg.
0401	A/Co. 084 deg.
0530	Co. 083 deg.
0631	Cape B——z 149 deg. 22,300 yards.
0700	A/Co. 093 deg.
0853	Increased speed to 18 knots.
0906	A/Co. 310 deg., to land on 2 A/C. (Aircraft).
0912	A/Co. 096 deg. 0918 Speed 15.
0930	Damietta W/T masts 174 deg., 13 miles.
0938	A/Co. 120 deg.
1112	Speed 17. 1116 Speed 15.
1145	Channel buoy abeam to port 3 cables. A/Co. 201 deg. HMS Verulum proceeded independently.

Post Meridian.

1205	Special Sea Duty Men and Cable Party.
1245	Hands fall in. – Prepare to moor station buoys.
1250	approx. Pilot embarked.
1258	Passed Boom, courses and speeds as requisite for proceeding to E3 Berth. Port Said Harbour.
1336	Let go port anchor, ship brought up to 1 shackle in 6 fathoms. Cables secured as requisite for securing ship in E3 Berth between head and stern buoys.
1400	Ship secured.
1440	Commenced fuelling from ashore. 2 water boats secured port side.
1515	Ammunition lighter secured alongside.
1540	White watch to muster, embark ammunition.
1630	Red and White watches employed ammunitioning and embarking victualling stores.
1650	S/Lt.(A) GOLDRING RNVR discharged to hospital.
1730	Completed fuelling, 361 tons of fuel oil and 18 tons of diesel embarked.
1800	Lighters cast off.

1801	Sunset.
2050	rating discharged to HMS STAR.
2200	Pipe Down.

Wind: NW.
Temperature: 60deg.
Barometric pressure: 1024.
Number on sick list: 6.

19th. March 1945 – Log Book Record (Port Said to Port Suez).

Ante Meridian.

0050	2 ratings joined ship.
0500	Called all hands.
0530	Hands fall in, single up wires, 2 Suez Canal Company pilots embarked.
0545	Special Sea Duty Men and Cable Party.
0610	Weigh anchor.
0618	Anchor aweigh, slip and proceeded through Suez Canal, courses and speeds as required.
0745	Hands fall in – clean ship.
0850	Hands fall in, normal harbour routine.
1110	Passed Ismalia, exchanged pilots.
1150	Secure.

Post Meridian.

1620	Disembarked mooring boats.
1630	Cleared Canal, proceeded to anchorage, courses and speeds as requisite.
1646	Let go starboard anchor, ship brought up to 3 shackles in 9 fathoms.
1655	Disembarked pilots.
1710	Fall out special sea duty men and cable party.
1730	Blue watch of hands to muster, disembark empty ammunition cases.
1740	Lighter secured alongside port side forward.
1800	Sunset.
1810	Blue watch secured, cast off lighter.
0230	Pipe Down.

Wind: W or Light Airs.
Temperature: 65 degrees.
Barometric pressure: 1024.
Number on sick list: 6.

I must confess to being somewhat taken aback by the trip through the Suez Canal; I expected something similar to the canals of England. Nothing could be further from the truth – there were, for example, vast expanses of sand and there were no locks, the water between the Mediterranean and the Red Sea being level throughout and, although lengths of the canal were narrow and similar to our canals, the stretch from Port Said to Suez contained lakes, the largest being the Great Bitter Lake, very useful as 'passing' points. Our navigation along the canal was tricky at times, there being barely room for a ship of our size to fit between the banks. Nevertheless, our journey along this 174 km., stretch of water was peaceful and tranquil, the Hun having been chased north long ago.

SUEZ CANAL

A ship canal cut through the Isthmus of Suez to connect the Mediterranean to the Red Sea. Long before it was established, a small canal existed, using intervening lakes, constructed in the time of Seti I (1380 BC), and is referred to in inscriptions in the Temple of Karnak; it remained in use until AD 770. The first planning of the modern canal dates from Napoleon's expedition to Egypt in 1798.

In 1846 the Societe d'Etudes pour le Canal de Suez was founded by Prosper Enfantin, and did much preliminary work in surveying the route and geological strata. On November 30th. 1854, Said Pasha, viceroy of Egypt granted to Ferdinand de Lesseps a concession for the construction of the canal, and the Compagnie Universalle du Canal Maritime de Suez was formed with a capital of £8,000,000 in 400,000 shares of £20 each, but the shares were not well taken up, particularly in England, where the scheme had all along been opposed on both political and technical grounds, the issue being saved from failure by Said Pasha. There were continuing difficulties, not least of all financial, but the canal was opened on 17th. November 1869. The length of the canal is 103 miles, including the approach channels; 21 miles are in lakes Balah and Timsa, and the Great Lakes.

SUEZ

A town situated at the south end of the Suez Canal and on the Gulf of Suez, gave its name to an administrative area. In the neighbourhood were the Wells of Moses, situated on the East side of the gulf. Fresh water was obtained from the Nile at Cairo by the Ismailia canal. Railways connected the town with Cairo, Port Said and with Port Ibrahim at the southern entrance of the canal. (Population: 108,250). The Gulf of Suez, part of the Red Sea, lay between the Sinai peninsular and Egypt. Its length was about 190 miles, with an average width of 30 miles.

The entrance to Port Said and the Canal on the outward journey.
Aircraft crammed on the Flight Deck.

Suez Canal.

Suez Canal showing the sandy banks.

The Red Sea must be taken as read(!) there being no memories of note to report. At the south end of the Red Sea was the port of Aden, a British key possession in the Middle East, and a useful stopping-off point for Royal Naval vessels, there being a sizeable harbour. This town (port) and territory, situated near the entrance to the Red Sea, was built on a volcanic peninsular of the same name, 5 miles long by 3 miles broad and 105 miles east of the Straits of Bab-el-Mandeb. It was an important and strongly fortified coaling station and port of call for P. & O. and other liners on the seaway to and from India, having been a fresh significance by the construction of the Suez Canal. On an isthmus connecting Aden to the

Passing mail during the passage through the Red Sea.

Aden.

mainland were four salt works, the salt being extracted from the seawater. It also boasted a cable and wireless station. The climate was hot but not unhealthy and water was scarce, being piped from the wells near Sheikh Othman through a 15 inch pipe, 6 miles in length. Practically all foodstuffs had to be imported.

Before leaving Aden, it is worth mentioning that the settlement had an area of 75 square miles and a population of about 48,500. A command of the R.A.F. was established at Aden in 1928 and, during the Second World War, the area became the base for attacks on Italian East Africa, 1940 –1941.

Bombay lay nearly 2,000 miles in a easterly direction from Aden, and the journey from Suez to Bombay had taken from 20th. March to 28th. March with very little to report. When a Royal Navy ship was sailing at a steady speed across a stretch of water such as the Arabian Sea during the war, routine was important to maintain discipline and effectiveness, although at this juncture in World War II, the possibility of engaging with the enemy was negligible.

BOMBAY

Bombay was sometimes referred to as, 'The Manchester of India', and that gave some idea of its nature. It was situated on the island of Bombay and was the capital of the province of Bombay and the chief seaport of Western India, with the title 'Gateway of India', that was symbolised in the memorial pavilion of yellow basalt stone. It was erected during the governorship of Lord Willingdon to commemorate the landing there of King V and Queen Mary in 1911. The island was linked to the island of Salsette in the north by a causeway that carried the railway to the mainland. Bombay Island was 11 miles long from Colaba in the south to Sion, where the causeway began, and from 3 to 4 miles broad in the middle. It had an area of 22.48 square miles. The climate was tropical without extreme heat and with an average rainfall of about 70 inches.

From the sea could be seen many fine buildings in their setting of tall palms fringing the Back Bay, giving a pleasant impression of 'modern' oriental splendour. The harbour on the other side of the island was one of the finest in the East. Possessing a university, a cathedral that shows a mixture of Classical and Gothic styles, two main railway termini, one of India's leading newspapers (Times of India), a legislature and a municipal corporation dating from 1888, Bombay maintained its position as a great port, an industrial centre and a leading contributor to India's history. In recent years the city and docks had been the scene of frequent disorders, of which some mutinous demonstration by sailors of the R.I.N. in February 1956 ranked amongst the more serious. Cotton has played a large part in India's prosperity and in Bombay Island there were 2,900,000 spindles and 66,000 looms.

Bombay: 1. The Gateway of India. 2. The Taj Mahal Hotel. 3. The Pydhonie Mosque. 4. The Victoria Railway Terminal.

Cochin, South India.

We were allowed ashore for a short time, a great relief after so many days at sea and out of sight of land. I had the opportunity to walk through the arch, 'The Gateway of India'. It reminded me to somewhat of the 'Arc de Triomphe' in Paris.

Leaving Bombay and wishing that more time could have been spent there (there was, of course, a war on!), we proceeded south to a little place called Cochin, not far from the southern tip of India. It was the chief port of the Malabar coast of southwest India and was, incidentally, the first European settlement of India, colonised by the Portuguese in1502. Exports included coconut oil and coir, and tea from Travancore.

I cannot remember why we stopped at Cochin, and no shore leave was granted.

The next trip was to be a short one, just round the 'corner' to Ceylon, now called Sri Lanka, first to Colombo, where shore leave would be granted and then to the other side, the east side of the island, namely Trincomalee. We were to discover that Trincomalee, the naval base, was ideal for swimming.

Chapter Three

FROM BOMBAY TO SYDNEY

On checking my route map, I see that we went to Ceylon before visiting Cochin, but I cannot give any reason for doubling back on our tracks. Our first port of call was Colombo on the west coast of Ceylon, where we were able to go ashore and explore to some extent, although there was not a great deal to see. But then, we did not venture very far, shore leave not being all that long. Incidentally, it was the 1st.April 1945, one month since leaving Greenock, Scotland. I estimate that we have covered approximately 12,500 miles or about a fifth of our round trip of 60,000 miles.

COLOMBO

The capital of Ceylon and its chief port. It had a large artificial harbour and was an important naval base and the administrative and trade centre of the island. The business quarter lay at the south end of the harbour, where the governor's residence, Queen's House government buildings, and the principal hotels were situated. Further on was the lake and beyond it was the Victoria Park, which contained the Colombo Museum, while between the lake an the sea was a narrow isthmus, Galle Face, where there were promenades and recreation grounds. Victoria Park was the centre of the residential quarter. Colombo boasted two cathedrals near the harbour and hospitals near Campbell Park. The town was lit by gas and electricity and there were electric

Colombo, Ceylon (now Sri Lanka).

tramways. The water supply came from a reservoir in the hills some 30 miles away. There were factories and stores in connection with the planting industry. The harbour was of recent date, the first breakwater, 4,200 feet long, having been completed in 1884. The port had a first class graving dock. It belonged to the Portuguese from 1517 to 1656, when it became Dutch. It became British in 1796. The population included, Tamils, Malays, and a number of mixed Portuguese and Dutch descent, and totalled 284, 155.

Colombo, Ceylon, through a porthole.

As I mentioned earlier, after Colombo we popped back to Cochin (India) for no reason that I can remember, returning to Ceylon, but this time to Trincomalee on the other side of the island from Colombo.

TRINCOMALEE

A seaport on the north east coast of Ceylon. It was built on a peninsula separating the outer from the inner harbour in the Bay of Trincomalee. The inner harbour was about 4 square miles in area and deep enough to take the biggest ships. For a long time the head quarters of the East India squadron, it was later used only as an oil depot and a subsidiary base to Singapore. While Singapore was in Japanese hands, 1942-45, Trincomalee again became a British naval base and was heavily bombed by Japanese carrier-borne aircraft on 9th. April 1942. The ships in port, when the attacking force was sighted, put to sea; Dorsetshire, completed in 1929, which sank the Bismark, and Cornwall, completed in 1927, which sank the German raider Pinguin in the Indian Ocean in 1941, and the 10,500 ton aircraft carrier Hermes were sunk by air attack some 10 miles off shore. A large number of the crew members were saved. Into Trincomalee Bay flowed the Mahaweliganga, the biggest river of Ceylon. Population 20,000.

Ceylon, now Sri Lanka, has been in turmoil for much of the latter part of the last century.

My one regret about our visit to Ceylon was that, whilst ashore, I was not able to drink a cup of tea!

3rd. April 1945 – Colombo, Ceylon to Cochin, S. West India. Log Book Record.

0800	Colours.
0815	Colours half-masted.
0830	HMS Ceylon flying C.S.5 flag entered harbour.
0900	Colours re-hoisted. HMS Royalist entered harbour.
0920	1 rating discharged to HMS Landa.
0950	Naval stores boat secured star'd side aft.
1105	Naval stores boat cast off.
1350	Cable Party and Special Sea Duty Men.
1355	Pilot aboard. 1410 Let go aft.
1415	Heave in both anchors.
1441	Star'd anchor aweigh.
1447	Port anchor aweigh. Ship under way.
1500	Pilot disembarked.
1518	Co. 028 degrees. Speed 17 knots – proceeded down swept channel.
1552	'S.C.1' abeam to port; a/c to 306 degrees.
1600	Commenced Zig Zag No. 38.
1630	Clear Lower Deck. Captain addressed ship's company.
1825	a/c 285 degrees.
1925	Sunset.
1930	Closed up Defence Watch.
	Distance travelled: 135 miles.
	Wind: SW and W.
	(It would seem the only reason that we
	visited Cochin was to replenish our stores.)
	Temperature: 80 degrees.
	Barometric pressure: 1009.
	Number on sick list 8.

The next chapter in our trip to the Pacific involved a big hop across the Indian Ocean and round the southern shores of Australia to Sydney, a mere 6,526 miles! The monotony of another two weeks at sea, much of it out of sight of land, was not a matter to ignite great enthusiasm, but again daily routine and regular duties, organised to keep the ship's company on its toes, prepared us for what lay ahead in our trips from Sydney up to the main fleet off Japan. There was, of course, the prospect of the 'Crossing the Line' ceremony, something that I had already experienced whilst a crew member of HMS Beagle.

CROSSING THE LINE

I have tried to establish the origins of this ceremony, how it came in to being and why, but without success. Setting up the ritual is important and requires a volunteer to act the part of Neptune, other crew members to offer to act as his minions. A pool of water has to be established on board with a ducking stool on the side. A large wooden razor forms part of the ritual together with a plentiful supply of soapsuds. A small number of the crew are selected to be inducted by King Neptune into the large number of sailors who have already 'crossed the line', and they in turn sit on the stool, are lathered with the soapsuds, shaved with the razor and tipped into the pool. All the members of the crew, on each particular voyage crossing the

'Crossing the Line' ceremony. Top: shaving. Middle: dipping. Bottom: finale.

equator, are issued with certificates signed by Neptune - I happen to have two, having already 'crossed the line' on HMS Beagle. The accompanying photographs give some idea of this fun situation, with individuals dressed for the individual parts acted out; my own certificate was signed by the members of the Radar complement aboard HMS Arbiter.

'*Crossing the Line*' *ceremony – certificate.*

After negotiating the southern shores of Australia, we approached Sydney, our base for the Pacific War area, bypassing Canberra the capital before entering the expansive entrance to the harbour – we were to view the Sydney Harbour Bridge for the first time, long before the Opera House was even thought about. There is a photograph in the book showing HMS Arbiter dwarfed by the bridge (page 28).

SYDNEY

The capital of New South Wales. It was the principal port and chief fortified naval station of the Australian Commonwealth, commercial and shipping centre for the South Pacific, an important international airport, extending 4 miles north and south by 3 miles east and west on the picturesque shores of Port Jackson, one of the finest natural harbours in the world. The mother city of the island continent, it was founded on January 26th. 1788 by Captain A. Phillip, six days

Entering Sydney Harbour with the appropriately dressed members of the crew lining the flight deck as a mark of respect.

after he had landed at Botany Bay, and was named after Thomas Townshend, First Viscount Sydney (1733-1800), who suggested the colonisation of New South Wales, and he was colonial secretary when the territory became a British possession. Population (1947) 1,484,434.

The site of the old town, 5 miles from the harbour entrance at the head of Sydney Cove, was chosen because it was near a limpid stream of water, long since covered in, and then, or soon after called the Tank stream. The original irregular and narrow streets were being replaced rapidly by fine buildings, spacious gardens and wide thoroughfares. The total street mileage of the city proper was over 134 miles, with suburban streets totalling 2,050 miles. The entrance to the harbour, nearly 1 mile across between Middle Head and Inner South Head, faced N.N.E.

The harbour extended 13 miles inland and covered an area of 13,600 acres, or 21 square miles, with a coastline of 188 miles. The coastline was so indented that the wharves, 14 miles of them, were close to the centre of the city.

HMS Arbiter dwarfed by Sydney Harbour Bridge.

Named after Sir George Jackson (1725-1822), secretary to the British admiralty, Sydney harbour is geologically a 'drowned valley', has no large rivers bringing down silt, and has a depth of water at the heads of 80 feet, and at the wharves of from 30 feet to 50 feet. The tidal rise and fall ranges from 3 feet to 6

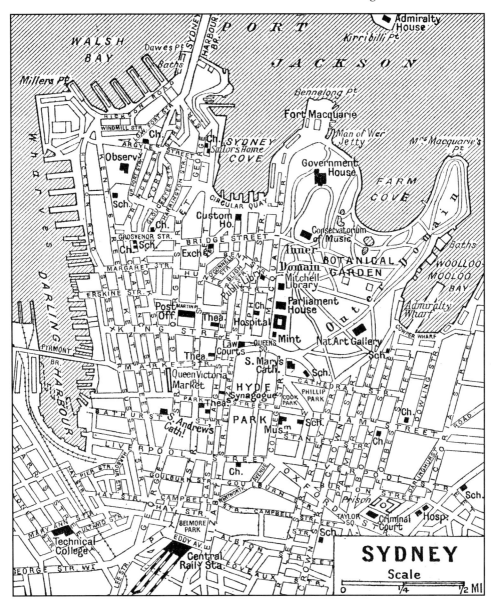

A map of Sydney.

feet, with an average of 3 feet 4 inches. In the fairway is a reef running parallel to the direction of the incoming and outgoing vessels, leaving two channels of 40 feet or more at low water. At least fifty vessels the size of the Queen Elizabeth could be comfortably accommodated at one time in the harbour. During World War II, from January 1945, Sydney was the head quarters of the British Pacific Fleet. The bridge across the harbour was opened in March 1932, and is nearly 3 miles long, including the approaches, with the central span of 1,650 feet. It cost £9,700,000 and contains 52,300 tons of steel. Its deck, 160 feet wide, gave a clearance for shipping of 170 feet.

Peter Ward ashore in Sydney.

There were several graving docks, including the Captain Cook Graving Dock, opened in 1945, which could take the largest vessel afloat. There were also a number of floating docks and patent slips, an extensive loading and unloading facility together with a coaling plant, not forgetting facilities for storing and loading grain in bulk. The wharves were in private hands until 1901, when the harbour trust was formed. The Sydney harbour authority's annual revenue was £1,380,000. In 1946-47, 3,628 vessels entered, with a net tonnage of 5,836,808; cargo totalled 9,033,487 tons – the heaviest to that date was handled in the year ending June 30th. 1945. The light at the harbour entrance was visible for 30 miles.

There were two main cathedrals, the metropolitan cathedral of St. Andrew and the Roman Catholic cathedral of St. Mary. Other buildings include some 200 churches, the Jewish synagogue, government offices, the town hall (with a fine organ), a technical college, government house, a post office, mint, observatory, art gallery, public libraries, museums, the central railway station, markets, schools, hospitals, the conservatorium of music etc. There were many parks, squares and public gardens. Water in abundance was obtained from the

Nepean River. Transport included underground railway, tram and ferry systems. Coal was obtained from mines less than 100 miles distant. Manufactures included clothing, boots and shoes, pottery, glass, furniture, tobacco, carriages, stoves, distilleries, breweries and machine shops.

Sydney was a favourite tourist resort with its own government tourist bureau, its harbour providing a delightful picnic ground for holiday-makers; bays and bathing beaches marked the many miles of its wooded foreshores, and glorious panoramic views of rugged headlands could be obtained from almost any point of its coastline. Mean temperature ranged from 72 degrees Fahrenheit in January to 53 degrees F. in July. Mean annual rainfall was 46.46 inches.

I may say at this point that I have happy memories of Sydney, but because we did not spend lengthy periods of time in the harbour, I was not able to partake of as many of the facilities mentioned earlier as I would have like to have done, but more of that anon. Suffice to say that Sydney was our operational base for the Pacific War Zone, from which we were to visit the Philippines, Hong Kong etc., during our task of keeping the main fleet off Japan supplied with aircraft, supplies etc.

2nd. May 1945. Sydney Harbour, Australia. Typical Log Record.

Number 4 Berth, Woolloomooloo.

	Red and White Watches shore leave: 1600-1700
	Ch. and P.O.'s. 0730.
0530	Called Air Department. Ordinary Rates under 20: 2200.
	Air Department: 1900-0700.
0600	Called the remainder of the Hands. Ch. and P.O.'s. 0730.
0625	All Watches of the Hands fall in.
0645	Special Sea Duty men close up. Pilot on board.
0652-0655	Tugs secured for'd and aft.
0750	White Watch to Defence Stations. Passed through West Gate of Boom.
0752	Pilot left. Fall out Special Sea Duty men.
0910	Stop engines. Commence flying off aircraft by catapult.
1050	Flying completed.
1100	Special Sea Duty men and Cable Party close up.
1210	Pilot on board.
1230	Passed the West Gate of the Boom and proceeded up harbour to No.4 Berth Woolloomooloo. Courses and speeds as requisite for going alongside.

1355	Secure head and astern. Wires doubled up.
1404	Fall out Special Sea Duty men.
1530	Secure.
1615	Power lighter secured alongside.
1715	Sunset.
1820	S/L's. Thornton, Schwenger and Brown, and 1 Petty Officer discharged to hospital.
1930	Squadron personnel left the ship – 141 Officers and Ratings.
2155	Pipe Down.

Temporary Sub. Lieut. (Sp. Br.) V.K. Luton R.N.V.R. was cautioned on account of his behaviour on shore on the night of Thursday 3rd.May. (Entry on wrong day!).
Wind: Light Airs.
Temperature: 65 degrees.
Barometer: 1018.
No. on sick list: 13.

3rd. May 1945. Sydney Harbour, Australia. Typical Log Record.

Number 4 Berth Woolloomooloo.

0615	Call the Hands.
0745	All Watches of the Hands employed on part-ship duties.
0800	Colours.
0915	Commence embarking oil fuel.
1010	61 Engine Room ratings joined the ship.
1150	Secure.
1410	Oil fuelling completed – 920 tons.
1700	Duty Watch employed embarking stores.
1715	Sunset.

Red and White Watches shore leave granted 1600 – 0700.
Ch. & Po's. 0730. Watch keepers 1300 – 0800.

| 2200 | Pipe Down. |

Wind: light airs.
Temperature: Low 60's degrees.
Barometric pressure: 1019 average.
Number on sick list: 15.

9th. May 1945. No.4 Berth, Woolloomooloo, Sydney. Typical Log Record.

0615   Called the Hands.

0745   All watches of the hands employed part of ship duties.

0810   Colours.

0900   Hands to clean.

0930   Hands to Divine Service – V.E. Day.

1150   Secure – No.4 Berth, Woolloomooloo.

1240   HMS Implacable entered Sydney Harbour.

1300   Duty watch employed bringing on stores.

1600   2 Ratings joined the ship.

1709   Sunset.

2200   Pipe Down.

       Leave for Red and White watches: 1230 – 0700.

       Usual watch-keepers leave.

Sydney harbour entrance.

A view of Sydney.

For leave purposes and for ship's duties, the whole crew were divided into groups, sometimes two groups called 'Port' and 'Starboard', and sometimes three groups called 'Red', 'White' and 'Blue'. This created two possible organisations of the crew, thus providing a flexible system, ready for any eventuality. It also meant that each member of the crew was dealt with fairly as far as duties and leave were concerned. Everybody knew exactly what was expected of them, and this was particularly important in the event of 'Action Stations', a state of alert in the face of the enemy, when everyone manned 'special duty' stations, each member of the crew having an individual responsibility that contributed to 'Arbiter's' effectiveness.

At one point during our trips from Sydney to the main fleet via Manus, The Admiralty Islands etc., we were tied up alongside in Sydney harbour for members of the crew to spend a fortnight with an Australian family. To cater for the organisation required to find homes for considerable numbers of sailors, the Australian authorities had set up Hospitality Centres, and it was to one of these that I duly reported. The Holiday Hut, as it was called, was run by Anne Marsh a volunteer organiser, and was situated in Queen's Square (the top of King Street, opposite Hyde Park). I was given a card on which was the following invitation

Harvey Bay: a plane dropping mail on the flight deck.

– 'You are cordially invited and will be welcomed at my home to spend your leisure time during the next few days. Here is my address: 'Pineleigh', No.666, Forest Road, Mortdale. Instruction on how to get there followed: 'Train from St. James to Hurstville. Leave station on right, take bus to 108, Peakhurst right to the door'. Looking forward to the pleasure of your company, Mr. And Mrs. Wales. As far as I can recollect, one other member of the crew accompanied me.

In fact 'Pineleigh was a farm, and the 'Wales's' had two children, a boy and a girl. The family couldn't have been more hospitable, with barbeques etc., the weather being just right for out-door activities. There were horses on the farm and one of the things that intrigued me was the fact that the children, when riding them, just hopped on the back of the chosen horse without bothering to saddle up, that is, bareback! Yours truly, always having had a streak of bravado in his nature, decided that what they did was common practice on the farms and that anyone could do it. Besides the streak of bravado there was also a modicum of sanity and so, the choice of time to try this out was important – an audience was out of the question.

Early one morning when nobody was outside and as they were busy doing other things, I stole into the paddock and chose what looked to me as the most docile animal. I hopped on its back fairly easily, the horses were not very big, and guided the animal out through the gate into the lane. All was going well until I started to slip sideways. Oh how I wished for a saddle. I hung on to the horse's neck, but of no avail. You might say that I was in control to a certain extent in so far that the horse and I had not parted company, but the connection was tenuous as I found myself under the horse's head looking into its mouth and hanging on like grim death as we proceeded down the lane, but not for long. I decided that wisdom was the better part of valour and I managed to make contact with the ground with my feet, the horse and I parting company for the better. I sheepishly led the animal back into the paddock, marching nonchalantly back into the farmhouse kitchen asking what

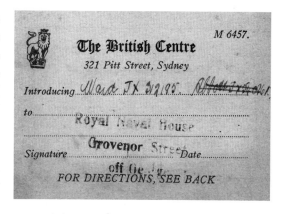

A card from the British Holiday Centre.

A card showing the directions to the farm in the Blue Mountains.

was for breakfast! I trust that you as the reader of this book will keep my secret of 60 years in order to spare my blushes. The experience taught me how useful saddles can be, even though the children rode bareback so effortlessly and so naturally, but they had been doing it from an early age, and it did save them all the paraphernalia of saddling up each time they had the urge to ride.

My memories of Australia and the people living there are pleasant ones and, at the time, it seemed the ideal place to live. I was young and lacking any real experience of life, so once I was back in England after being demobbed, the thoughts quickly faded. Another pleasant memory worth mentioning was my introduction to ice-skating. I think the ice rink was called the 'Silver Blades' and I found I had a certain natural aptitude, unlike riding bareback!

Chapter Four

BACKGROUND TO THE BRITISH OPERATION IN THE PACIFIC WAR

On the 28th. September 1944, Mr. Winston Churchill, then Prime Minister of Great Britain, told the House of Commons, "The new phase of the war against Japan will command all our resources from the moment the German war is ended. We owe it to Australia and New Zealand to help them remove forever the Japanese menace to their homeland and, as they helped us on every front in the fight against Germany, we will not be behindhand in giving them effective aid. We have offered the fine modern British Fleet and asked that it should be employed in the major operations against Japan. For a year past modern battleships have been undergoing modification and tropicalisation to meet wartime changes in technical apparatus. The scale of our effort will be limited only by available shipping."

On the 17th. December 1944, less than three months afterwards, the Royal Navy began implementing that promise; nearly five months before the German war had ended. On that day the 35,000 battleship HMS Howe sailed into Sydney harbour, wearing the flag of Admiral Bruce Fraser, Commander-in-Chief of the newly formed Pacific Fleet. Then came other units, including HMS King George V, Flagship of Vice-Admiral Sir Bernard Rawlings, HMS Indomitable, Flagship of Vice-Admiral (then Rear-Admiral) Sir Philip Vian, two other famous carriers, HM Ships Illustrious and Victorious, a cruiser squadron commanded by Rear-Admiral Eric Brind, flying his Flag in HMS Swiftsure, and a large destroyer force under the command of Rear-Admiral John Edelsten.

On the way to Australia, most of these ships had engaged the Japanese in a preliminary encounter by striking at enemy oil-fields in Sumatra.. To most of the ships' companies Australia was a strange place on the other side of the world, a land of cricketers and Kangaroos, of desert and drought, of vast sheep farms and sunny beaches, a few large cities, and certainly of tough fighting men. As they stepped ashore for the first time, our men found a home from home, not so surprising bearing in mind the backgrounds of the two countries, and a welcome unequalled in any of the world's ports where British ships have called. The men in the streets shook hands and the girls smiled pleasantly. The men in the pubs bought beer, scarce though that homely refreshment was. Motorists pulled up at street corners and sailors were invited to their homes. To the ships came hundreds of invitations to dances and parties and to spend leave in Australian homes – my own personal experience of this generosity is described on another page – and on the sheep stations. The sun shone, the shops were full of good things, and food was plentiful and excellent. It was a grand place and a grand welcome.

While British sailors enjoyed this smiling land of sunshine and comparative plenty (their two breakfast eggs were equivalent to two month's ration at home!), they also had to prepare their ships for the new warfare. With Sydney the main base, fighting would be 4,000 miles away. So the first aim was to establish a base. An early development was the setting up of Mobile Operational Naval Air Bases (Monabs), where aircraft could be assembled, serviced and flown to the carriers. HMS Arbiter played an important part in these operations.

The organisation required for the smooth running of the Pacific campaign was enormous and unique – nothing on this scale had been required in the past – one of the main problems being distances needing to be covered in supplying the Main Fleet off Japan with aircraft, ammunition, food etc. In Australia's ports administration, offices were set up, stores and warehouses opened, followed by ordnance and engineering shops that were soon noisy with work for the ships. The distractions of life ashore were only for the men off duty or on leave. The others worked at full stretch on guns and torpedo tubes, engines and boilers, radar sets and signalling apparatus, making sure that all was ready for Britain's new offensive. Helping the Navy were thousands of civilians, girl clerks and typists in offices, storekeepers, riveters, welders and dockers. To cope with the rush of work, additional installations were made. The mightiest of these was the Captain Cook graving dock at Garden Island, completed in time for most of the major units of the fleet to receive attention there. But the greatest problem of all was how to keep the Fleet at sea for the extended periods necessary if it was to operate continuously against the Japanese. The Fleet Train, commanded by Rear-Admiral Douglas Fisher, provided the answer; a gigantic sea-going caravan of tankers, and of store, repair and depot ships based variously at Manus in the Admiralty Islands, or in the Leyte Gulf in the Philippines. From there it was decided that food, clothing, medicine supplies, fuel, bombs, engine parts and that most important commodity of all, mail, should be sent to the fighting units at sea by sea. Aircraft were embarked on escort carriers like HMS Arbiter to replace battle losses and, attached to the Train, were hospital ships to care for the sick and wounded. Some ships lay in advanced anchorages for many sweltering weeks of tireless service for the Fleet, in humidity, heat and slashing rain, only a few degrees from the Equator. There were no amenities ashore and the only real exercise available was swimming. There is a photograph (page 44) of some of the crew of 'Arbiter' taking advantage of relaxing and exercising in the water at Manus (Admiralty Islands), accompanied by a whaler for safety reasons. It is probably worth mentioning that many of the crew had their hair cropped whilst in the Far East, that made it easier to cope with than normal long hair and was easier to keep clean.

Apart from radio and gramophone programmes broadcast over the ship's tannoy system (a broadcasting system by which the Captain, or anybody else, could address the ship's company - it was also used to sound 'action stations'), the men had to provide their own entertainment. Where was the glamour of the Pacific, the romantic nights, the heart-throb music of grass-skirted island beauties, or the long sunny days by blue lagoons? No British sailors found them in Manus, Leyte, Guam or Subie Bay. The names mean memories only of steaming days and dank, suffocating nights. Fortunately there was one strong link with the outside world, the mail. I remember mentioning in my first book, 'From Africa to the Arctic' (A Year aboard HMS Beagle), my amazement at receiving mail in various god forsaken places, but the powers that be knew how important this was for the morale of the fighting forces. For the sailors in the front-line ships out in the Far East, mail days were the week's highlights for the men of the Fleet Train. In Sydney the Fleet Mail Office, staffed largely by Wrens, strove to give efficient service, but none of their efforts could have succeeded without those airmen of the Transport Command. British sailors will always be grateful to them for making long, trying and often hazardous flights that enabled mail to be received regularly and in good time.

22nd. June 1945. Based at Manus, Admiralty Islands. Typical Log Record.

0530	Called the Hands.
0600	Special sea duty men and cable party close up.
0626	Anchor aweigh. Proceed out of harbour.
0640	Passed boom. Blue Watch to cruising stations.
0652	Fall out special sea duty men.
0710	Commenced speed trial.
0720	All Watches fall in. Clean ship.
0810	Speed trial completed.
0830	Special sea duty men.
0850	Entered Ponam harbour

0910	Let go Port anchor.
	Ship brought up to 4 shackles in 16 fathoms of water.
0915	Fall out special sea duty men.
1100	Disembarking aircraft.
1410	Special sea duty men and cable party. Red Watch to cruising stations.
1435	Anchor aweigh.
1500	Fall out special sea duty men.
1510	Commence Zig Zag 12.
1600	Exercise action stations.
1650	Action stations secure.
1720	Special sea duty men and cable party close up.
1733	Passed boom inwards.
1750	Let go Port anchor.
	Ship brought up to 5 shackles in 16 fathoms of water.
1810	Sunset.
2100	Rounds.
2215	Pipe down.
	Wind: Light airs.
	Temperature: 84 degrees.
	Barometric pressure: 1011.
	Number on sick list: 5.

23rd June 1945. Based at Manus, Admiralty Islands. Typical Log Record.

0545	Called the hands.
0700	Lt. Davidson U.S.N. rejoined ship.
0730	All Watches of the hands employed part of ship.
0800	Colours.
0830	Water boat alongside.
1010	Water boat cast off.
1020	Lt.Cdr. (A) Williams R.N. joined ship.
1813	Sunset.
2200	Rounds.
2225	Pipe down.
	Wind: am. E.S.E. pm. N.N.E.
	Temperature: 85 degrees.
	Barometric pressure: 1011.
	Number on sick list: 5.

THE STEADY ADVANCE TOWARDS JAPAN
– THE HAZARDS – THE CONTRASTS

I must go back a couple of months. On 28th. March 1945 began a two-month attack on the Sakishima Gunto, covering the southern flank of the American invasion of Okinawa. It was largely an operation for the fleet carriers because there was a need to bomb and strafe by cannon and rocket the airfields, ports and military installations. Bombardment was also carried out by battleships, cruisers and destroyers, but the main offensive burden fell on aircrews and the men who serviced their machines.

But the Japanese gave their punishment too. Because the attack from the air was so important, involving the mighty aircraft carriers, they became the prime target of the Japanese relentless, suicide plane attacks albeit, in the long term, hopeless. They were, nevertheless, a nightmare for the carriers and their crews, the Kamikaze attacks as they were known being a new kind of warfare, the planes plus their pilots being flown directly at the ships and doing immense damage, the Japanese pilots of course being killed. It was considered an honour by the Japanese to give their lives in the service of their country, something that the 'west' could never understand. HMS Arbiter was never part of the main fleet off Japan (we were part of the Fleet Train) and so escaped this sort of attack. First hand knowledge of this sort of warfare is therefore lacking, but accounts by those who suffered from it, tell horrendous stories and express the helplessness that they endured. Ships could only manoeuvre to try to avoid the attacking planes and use what armament was possible, sometimes successfully shooting down the oncoming 'flying bomb' before it hit its target. Throughout the Fleet, our men were kept at 'Action Stations' (on duty for as long as necessary) from dawn to dusk, sweating, always toiling and often very weary. I am led to believe that the Japanese pilot volunteers flew their planes with just enough fuel for them to reach their targets, making it impossible for them to return to their bases. Whether this was because of the shortage of fuel, whether the powers that be ordered it so, whether it meant more explosives could be carried, whether the pilots asked for it to be so, I do not know; possibly a combination of all these possibilities.

Relief from the strain of seemingly endless weeks at sea came when ships returned to Australia for repair. These were moments that the sailors looked forward to, as many Australian hosts and hostesses knew from letters written at sea. As the ships sailed into Sydney, Brisbane (which we were to visit at some point), Melbourne and other ports, countless eyes searched the shore for signs of friends. Their search was not in vain and the welcome, if anything, warmer. I doubt if anyone knows the full story of the Australian hospitality, but the work of Sydney's British Hospitality Centre may be acceptable as symbolic. There were 6,000 meals served daily, 1,200 beds provide nightly, each night 300 young women attended dances as hostesses, 63,000 were on the roster for this duty, and more than 4,000 voluntary workers shared the general work of the Centre. Day to day hospitality was offered in 12,5000 homes, where more than 80,000 men were entertained in New South Wales alone – I was one of them of course, as described in another chapter.

Operations in the North were not the only activities of the Royal Navy in the Pacific. Truk Island was raided in June, British submarines harried (and sank) what shipping they could find, and midget submarines (XE craft) penetrated defences to attack ships thought to be safe behind the boom. The submarine's work was little known until the closing stages of the war, but the extent to which it was appreciated in Australia was revealed when thousands of visitors passed through some of the boats at Melbourne and Adelaide. This enthusiasm rivalled the welcome they had received at Perth and Freemantle months before, and submariners claim that Western Australian hospitality surpassed even the best efforts of the other states.

HMS Arbiter made two trips up to the main Fleet during its time in the Pacific theatre of World War II, using Leyte (Philippines) and Manus (Admiralty Islands) as stopping-off points, although Manus was the main point of call in our two round trips to the British Fleet off Japan. The Americans had long since chased the Japanese out of Manus (as they had also done at Leyte), so we, at no time, came face to face with the enemy, which included, as mentioned earlier, the nightmarish scenario of the Japanese Kamikaze pilots. I cannot remember setting foot on either Leyte or Manus, which meant that a considerable amount of the time was spent at sea, with very little time on 'terra firma'. This made our visits to Sydney etc., all the more enjoyable.

Off-loading aircraft at Manus, Admiralty Islands.

British Pacific Fleet arriving at Manus – 'Arbiter' in the foreground.

Keeping the Fleet supplied with aircraft, ammunition, supplies and mail involved a number of different activities including passing people, mail etc., from one ship to another by a special contraption, slung from a rope or hawser linking the two vessels.

The rope was fixed to a bollard on one ship at one end, the other end being manned by a large number of sailors, pulling on it as if in a tug of war, thus keeping the rope reasonably taut without it breaking. This had to be done because of the unpredictability of the movement of the ships and in spite of them travelling in parallel and at the same speed. The photograph (page 48) shows this activity in action, with crew members of the 'Arbiter' manning the moving end of the rope – it was usual for the

An Avenger flying off prior to us arriving at Manus.

larger of the two vessels to be responsible for the unfixed end of the rope, with the destroyer on the receiving end. This manoeuvre was taking place in the 'forward area' off Japan. Other photographs shows oiling at sea, during which the vessel supplying the oil, usually an oil tanker, proceeds at an agreed speed, followed by the vessel requiring oil, travelling at the same speed and in an identical direction, the latter being responsible for any deviation.

Off-loading aircraft on to a floating platform, to be transported ashore, took place at Manus, and a photograph of this can be seen, with a Corsair in mid-air and part of the 'Arbiter' in the top right-hand corner (page 42). With us being many hundreds of miles north of Australia, I presume that the aircraft were able to fly to the Aircraft Carriers of the main Fleet off Japan. There is another picture showing the BPF Fleet arriving at Manus, with HMS Arbiter in the foreground.

Having said elsewhere that, owing to lack of first-hand experience, I have made scant reference to the American contribution to the downfall of Japan, bearing in mind that we were able to use Leyte as a base, I feel bound to mention some of the details of its capture. General Kruegar's U.S. 6th. army went ashore at Leyte on 20th. October 1944 and, within a few hours of their first landings in the Tacloban area of Leyte, the Americans had over 100,000 men ashore. The Japanese navy made desperate efforts to interfere with U.S. transports bringing reinforcements, but the virtual elimination

1. HMS King George V (battleship). 2. Swimming at Manus. 3. Ships of the Pacific Fleet at Manus. 4. HMS Implacable refuelling off Japan.

of the Japanese warships in the sea battles of October 23rd. - 27th. prevented any large-scale Japanese reinforcements. All organised Japanese resistance on Leyte ended on 25th. December 1944. Incidentally, the capture of Leyte cost the U.S. forces, 2,623 killed and 8,422 injured; the Japanese lost 113,221 men. On July 5th. MacArthur announced that, of the 450,000 Japanese in the Philippines, all but 30,000 men had been annihilated; 17 U.S. divisions had been engaged, and casualties were 54,891, of whom 11,021 had been killed. Lt.-Gen. Tomoyuki Yamashita the 'tiger of Malaya', conqueror of Corregidor and of Singapore ('Arbiter' paid a flying visit to Singapore on the way home), unconditionally surrendered himself and all remaining Japanese forces in the Philippines to Lt.-Gen. Wainwright (who, ironically, had surrendered to Yamashita at Corregidor), 3rd. September 1944.

ACCIDENTS CAN HAPPEN (I)

1. HMS Arbiter (British Pacific Fleet)
The following is an account of an accident involving fuelling, and the resultant recommendation for Honour and Awards.

RECOMMENDATION FOR HONOURS AND AWARDS – PERIODIC.

From: The Commanding Officer, H.M.S. Arbiter.

Date: 2 July, 1945.   No.07.

TO: COMMODORE COMMANDING
30TH AIRCRAFT CARRIER SQUADRON (5)

Recommendations for Honours and Awards on B.P.F.
Form Number 1 are forwarded herewith in respect of the following:

Chief Stoker H.B.Pascoe, D/K.65429
A.A. 3cl. B.A. McGale, FX.75150
Tempy. Sub-Lt.(E) H.W. Jackinson, R.N.V.R.
(Senior 4th. Engineer T.124X).

2. The recommendations are for courage and devotion to duty in saving the life during the accident in the petrol compartment of this ship, reported in Arbiter's Number 91 of 28th may, 1945.

3. Whilst HMS Arbiter was fuelling, a leak developed in the system and as petrol vaporised rapidly, the leak was not discovered at the time. On completion of fuelling, three ratings entered the petrol compartment to close the system and were overcome. They were discovered by Sub-Lt, Jackinson who went down, managed to bend (Ed. Tie) a rope on one of the ratings who was then hauled up, but was overcome himself. A.A. 3cl. McGale then entered the compartment, bent a rope on Sub-Lt. Jackinson who was hauled up but McGale was unable to attend to the other two ratings as he was himself overcome.

4. Chief Stoker Petty Officer Pascoe, wearing Salvas Breathing apparatus then entered the compartment, ascertained that there were two ratings remaining in the compartment (a fact which was uncertain at the time as Sub-Lt. Jackinson and McGale were still unconscious) and then had to come out as the Salvas Breathing Apparatus was not effective. Pascoe then donned Pattern 230 Self-breathing apparatus and fetched the remaining two ratings up; he was then overcome himself. One rating later died from his injuries.

5. The order of merit is as set out in paragraph 1 above.

Signed by the Captain – D.H. Everett.

(CAPTAIN, R.N.)

This is a copy (typed by the Author) of a document housed in the archives of the P.R.O. Kew.

ACCIDENTS CAN HAPPEN (II)

HMS Arbiter (British Pacific Fleet).

Following on the graphic description of the rescue made during the accident in the petrol compartment of HMS Arbiter, whilst operating in the Pacific on 23rd. May 1945 (Accidents can happen 1), an award was made to Temporary Stoker Petty Officer Havelock Bullock Pascoe, D/K.65429, details of which appeared in the London Gazette Supplement of 22nd. January 1946.
The wording was as follows.

28 January 1946.

Sir,

I am commanded by My Lords Commissioners of the Admiralty to inform you that they have learned with great pleasure that, on the advice of the First Lord, the King has been graciously pleased to award you the British Empire Medal (Military) for courage and devotion to duty in rescuing two men overcome by petrol fumes when a leak developed in a petrol compartment of H.M.S. Arbiter during operations in the Pacific on 23rd May 1945.

I am, Sir, Your obedient Servant,

(Signed)

Temporary Stoker Petty Officer Havelock Bullock Pascoe, D/K.65429.

This is a copy (typed by the Author) of a document housed in the archives of the P.R.O. Kew.

20th. July 1945. At sea, supplying the Main Fleet off Japan – Forward Area. (Typical Log Record)

0235	Altered Course to 210 degrees. 0247. A/c. to 240 deg.
0310	A/c. to 280 deg. 0348. Fleet sighted.
0455	A/c. to 280 deg. 9 knots.
0505	A/c. to 000 deg. 15 knots.
0507	8 knots. 0525. A/c. to 280 deg. 0535. A/c. to 255 deg.
0530	Call the Hands.
0728	Hauled out of line to fly off aircraft.
1114	1 Corsair took off for 'Victorious'.
1255	HMS Quality closed astern to oil.
1315	Commenced pumping.
1513	Ceased pumping.
1520	'Quality' cast off. 14 knots. Course 180 degrees.
1600	Transferred mail to WRANGLER.
1624	Corsair landed on.
1701	Corsair crashed on take-off. Catapulted eight Corsairs.

Forward Area – passing stores, mail etc. to a destroyer.

Forward Area – picture showing the method of passing objects between ships.

1748	Landed on 1 Corsair, 3 Corsairs and 1 Firefly.
1800	Entered screen. Course 255 degrees. 12 knots.
1802	'Termagent' alongside. 1850. Cast off.
2130	Pipe down.
2155	Took up position 005 degrees, 4000 yards from 'Indefatigable'.

Wind: W x S. (am) & W x N. (pm).

Position 0800: 31.59 N. - 151.02 E. (D.R.)

Temperature: mid 80's.

Position 1200: 31.21 N. - 150.33 E. (Sights)

Barometric pressure: 1012.

Position 2000: 31.50 N. - 149.27 E. (D.R.)

Number on sick list: 1.

Distance travelled: 197.5 miles.

Zone time: 9.

21st. July 1945. At sea - Forward Area. (Typical Log Record)

0530	Call the hands.
0550	Transferred stores to UNDAUNTED.
0642	Flew off Seafires.
0650	1 Seafire landed on – crashed into bridge.
0742	'Quality' alongside.
0740	Cast off.
0855	'Quality' alongside.
0905	'Quality' cast off.
0930	'Wakeful' alongside port side.
1005	'Urchin' alongside starboard side.
1010	'Urchin' cast off.
1058	'Wakefield' cast off.
1120	'Ulysses' alongside.
1128	Cast off.
1311	Proceed with NIZAM to MANUS as ordered.
	Alter course 220 degrees. (16 kts.)
1353	a/c.130 deg. 1357 a/c.160 deg. 1415 a/c.190 deg.
1439	a/c.158 deg. 1526 a/c.185 deg. 1540 a/c.190 deg.
1600	Commenced Zig Zag.
1800	Increased to 16.5 knots.
2000	Course 200 degrees.

2130   Pipe down.
2330   Clocks advanced 1 hour.
        Wind: N.E./Light air.
        Position 0800: 30.40 N. – 147.52 E. (D.R.)
        Temperature: 74 degrees.
        Position 1200: 30.34 N. – 147.60 E. (Sights)
        Barometric pressure: 1013.
        Position 2000: 28.57 N. – 146.50 E. (D.R.)
        Number on sick list: 1.
        Distance travelled: 276 miles.
        Zone time: 9.

6th. August 1945. At sea - Forward Area. (Typical Log Record)

0259   Alter course to 044 degrees.
0346   Alter course to 020 degrees.
0545   Courses and speeds as required to take up position to fly off aircraft.
0600   TEASER alongside with pilots.
0630   TEASER cast off.
0704   Catapulted one Avenger.
0745   Flew off ten Seafires.
0840   1 Avenger landed on.
0905   2 Seafires landed on.
0940   TEASER alongside.
1030   TEASER cast off.
1327   Three Corsairs catapulted.
1435   1 Firefly flown off.
1533   BARLE alongside.
1546   Cast off.
1550   URANIA alongside.
1600   Cast off.
1626   NIZAM alongside for fuelling.
        Position 0800: 35.00 N. – 147.00 E.
        Position 1200: 35.30 N. – 147.30 E.
        Position 2000: 36.20 N. - 146.48 E. (All Sights).
1640   Commenced pumping.
1808   Catapulted three Corsairs.
        Distance travelled: 217 miles. Zone 9

Forward Area – HMS Nizam refuelling.

HMS Nizam close-up.

1814	Ceased pumping. 102 tons of fuel transferred.
1904	NORMAN alongside with sailing orders.
1910	Cast off.
2000	Commenced forming until 112.2.51.
2225	Speed 10.5 knots.
2230	Pipe down.
	Course 210 degrees. Speed 10 knots.
	Wind: Light Air.
	Temperature: 75 degrees.
	Barometer: 1019.
	Number on sick list: 3.

7th. August 1945. At sea - Forward Area. (Typical Log Record)

0145	Reduced to 10 knots.
0953	Altered course to 270 degrees.
1020	Sighted HMS WOODCOCK, REDPOLE and ships in convoy.
1105	Altered course to 210 degrees.
1110	Altered course to 183 degrees. Speed 8 knots.
1219	Streamed hose for REDPOLE.
1240	Commenced pumping.
1320	Stopped pumping.
1350	REDPOLE cast off.
1345	REDPOLE alongside – transferred one cot case.
1400	REDPOLE cast off.
1550	REDPOLE alongside port side transferring stores.
1605	REDPOLE cast off.
1800	Left DINGLEDALE -
	REDPOLE and company proceeded ahead at 15/16 knots. Zone time: 9.
2330	Clocks advanced 1 hour. Zone time: 10.
	Wind: Light Air.
	Temperature: 75 degrees.
	Barometer: 1019.
	Number on sick list: 2.
	Distance travelled: 232 miles.
	Position 0800: 34.40.N. - 147.05 E. (Sights).
	Position 1200: 34.00 N. – 147.05 E. (Sights).
	Position 2000: 32.30 N. – 147.00 E. (Sights).

Week by week more ships came to the Pacific, transports brought fresh drafts to man them, until Churchill's 'fine modern British Fleet' was ranged off the shores of Japan for what was to have been the softening assault before invasion. It was a dramatic moment to be at the enemy's front door, to bomb his home airfields, to shell his home war plants and communications. Carrier personnel seldom were at rest as battleships and cruisers hurled broadsides at targets on shore. Busiest of all were the ever-watchful destroyers, alert for air, submarine, or suicide boat attack, but also ready for inshore bombardment.

The strain was tremendous, particularly for those who saw nothing of the drama as they sweated below in the engine and boiler room temperatures of 130 degrees Fahrenheit and more, to give the ships power – without the engine room, ships were powerless. Behind all were the Fleet Trains, always on the move. It is remarkable that the Fleet Trains were not attacked – only the Japanese know why! Certainly, attack was expected, and an escort group remained in formation for protection from that quarter. By crippling only the oil tankers, the Japanese could have crippled the Fleet. But they left the escort ships to keep monotonous watch, unrelieved by the activity of the fight.

The final chapter of the battle story of the British Pacific Fleet was written on 15th. August 1945. There were rumours that the enemy was about to surrender. Everybody hoped such was the case, but nobody relaxed on that account, and dawn found the usual air strikes over the Japanese mainland. The Fleet was still at Action Stations at 1100 when the signal was hoisted announcing the news that Mr. Atlee, Britain's new Prime Minister, had given the people at home......the enemy had surrendered (see page 91). The war was over, but not the task of the Fleet.

With the rest of the victorious Powers, Australia rejoiced. The aggressor had been broken and Australia could return to her job of making her place high among the nations of the world. But she rejoiced with certain reservations, there being thousands of her young men still in enemy hands. This situation applied to many nationalities, and 'Arbiter' played a part in returning people to 'Blighty'.

The Fleet cut short its victory celebrations (there is a photograph of the crew of HMS Arbiter on the flight deck being given the news by the captain, page 54) as its new job was to occupy Japanese territory, to free the prisoners of war and internees. Hospital ships were despatched to bring sick men home, aircraft carriers being fitted to help in the task – they were particularly appropriate with their vast hangars providing plenty of space.

At times it was tough going under difficult circumstances, but the job had been completed. Some men of the Fleet, notably those who came to the Pacific after fighting since that September day when the German war began, had gone

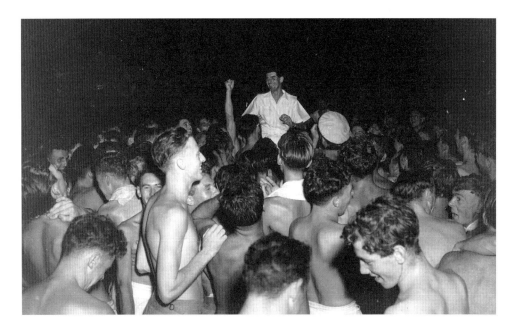

VJ Night – the Captain addressing the ship's company.

home, with most of the remainder due to follow, but some would stay to take up civil life in the land that made them welcome. In the jumbled thoughts that crowd a man's mind in wartime, many will have one outstanding memory, that of the hospitality and friendship they received when they set foot in Australia.

I have not included much of the contribution that the Americans and others made to the success of winning the war against the Japanese – it was of course enormous – but another book would do better justice to that part of the Second World War. Besides the argument for a separate book, I had no first hand experience of those theatres of the war. I have included, nevertheless, the retaking of Leyte etc., by the Americans, some time before 'Arbiter' visited it as one of the links in the Fleet Train.

During the long trips backwards and forwards from Sydney to the British Fleet off Japan, with lengthy periods at sea hundreds of miles from land, diversions were implemented. But more of that anon.

I cannot leave the crushing of the Japanese during the Philippines conflict without giving details of the decimation of the Japanese Fleet, the whole episode being an important contribution to the Allies success. I have already mentioned the vast human loss of life, but add to this the loss of three battleships, four aircraft carriers, six heavy cruisers, four light cruisers and nine destroyers, against the lesser losses of the US Navy i.e. one light aircraft carrier, two escort carriers and two destroyers. The losses devastated the Japanese Navy, although they still retained the three battleships, Yamato, Nagato and Haruna, but these were soon to follow the earlier losses, making the Imperial Japanese Navy virtually non-existent. A resultant plus meant that Leyte was available as a Naval Base, one visited by 'Arbiter' as well as Manus in the Admiralty Islands. General MacArthur had promised to return to the Philippines and, by the end of 1944, he had kept his promise.

Coming back to the diversions mentioned earlier, introduced to allay any possible boredom that might arise, although a strict regime was always in place to obviate this, one of the few recreational activities available to us was 'deck hockey'. It was arranged that different groups of members of the crew such as Radar, Signals, Stokers etc., play against each other, just for fun. The flight deck was pretty extensive, but even so, care had to be exercised to avoid large bills for balls lost over the side. The photograph shows a game in progress involving Radar personnel.

A signals cabin existed in the hangar, high up at the forward end so that it did not impede free movement of planes etc., and it was in there that I discovered a virtually unused 120 bass, Hohner Piano Accordion. I quickly discovered the patterns of knobs (chords etc.) played by the left hand and, being something of a pianist, found no difficulty with the keyboard, played by the right hand. I

Some of the Radar team playing deck hockey.

joined up with another couple of instrumentalists to form a trio, I seem to remember a clarinettist as one of the group, and being a signals office, we were able to perform over the tannoy (a public address system) to entertain the ship's company from time to time, mostly jazz and well known music. The acquisition of the skills necessary to play a Piano Accordion has come in useful over the years. This skill came in useful on the way home when the crew devised and performed a variety show for the passengers!

It was traditional, and I think still is, for the crew not actually attending to the duties necessary to running the ship, to line up on deck as a mark of respect. There is a photographed example of this as we entered Sydney Harbour, everybody dressed in tropical gear, suitable for the climate (page 27).

Unfortunately it became necessary from time to time to bury someone at sea, either because the individual had requested the tradition or because the ship was too far from land, a distinct possibility considering the mileage covered whilst keeping the Fleet off Japan fully supplied and active. Burial at sea followed a certain ritual, laid down in Naval Orders, and the photograph shows an example, the picture being a record for the family in their absence. The Chaplain usually officiated at the service.

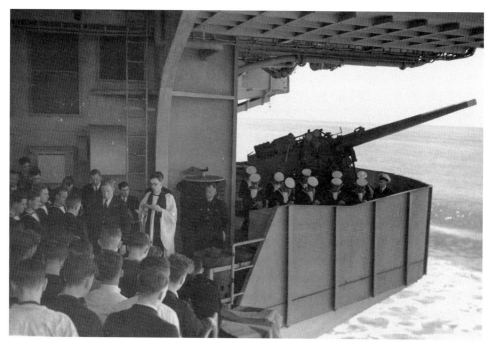

A burial at sea.

Chapter Five

A BRIEF VISIT TO BRISBANE

We made a brief visit to Brisbane towards the middle of September 1945, and although our stay could be measured in days, it was enough to see what a striking city it was. It was a pity that it was to be the only visit.

BRISBANE - the principal seaport, chief commercial centre and capital of Queensland, Australia. The city was built on a bend of the River Brisbane, 15 miles from its embouchure into Moreton Bay. It had a railway connection with Melbourne, Adelaide, Sydney and Perth, and was accessible to ocean-going vessels up to 25,000 tons. Three large bridges spanned the river.

The seat of a Roman Catholic archbishop and an Anglican bishop, Brisbane possessed several buildings of architectural merit, notably the parliament house,

HMS Arbiter at speed.

custom house, two cathedrals, Queensland Club, state treasury, supreme court, post office, city hall and museum. It was the seat of the university of Queensland, established by Act of 1909. A new university had been built. There were botanical gardens, a school of art, and several parks and open spaces. The aerodrome was one of the Commonwealth's finest. It was a well- planned city, with many buildings of skyscraper height.

Most of the residents lived in detached houses and 64 per cent owned their own homes. Roses bloomed all the year and flowering trees made city and suburbs a blaze of colour. Trade returns were principally from cattle, sheep, dairy produce, sugar and canned fruits. There, meat-processing works and the wharves, were thronged with freighters. It had the most equable climate of all the Australian capitals, with an average maximum temperature of 78 degrees and a minimum of 59 degrees Fahrenheit. Annual rainfall was 45 inches.

Occupied as a penal station in 1824 by Sir Thomas Brisbane, after whom it was named, Brisbane was opened to free settlement in 1842, and in 1859 became the colony's capital. In 1893 South Brisbane was almost wholly destroyed by flood. Population (est.) 384,000.

'Arbiter' and the sea by moonlight.

HMS Arbiter from the air.

We were en route from Brisbane to Sydney on the 14th. September, arriving there on the 15th. tying up alongside at 0735. Our stay in Sydney harbour on this occasion was only to last a few days, and on the 18th. we embarked oil and stores, leaving at 1750 on the 19th., this time heading for Manus (Admiralty Island). 'Arbiter' was, incidentally, heading for Hong Kong via Leyte. We were at sea during virtually the whole of the next ten days, negotiating the Jonnard Passage on September 23rd., safe passage being dependent on accurate course setting, stopping off at Manus on the 25th.

Leaving Manus on the 26th. with the clocks retarded by one hour (to coincide with Zone 9) on the 28th., we reached Leyte on the 30th. September for a brief visit, leaving at 0739 to head for Hong Kong. September 30th. must have been a Sunday, because the day included 'Hands to Church', which of course meant a religious service, also called 'Divisions'.

It is perhaps worth filling in some brief detail covering the early days of September, the first eight days involving the members of the crew in day-to-day

Divisions (a naval service) on Sunday 23rd. December 1945.

Another view of Divisions taking place.

duties. On the 8th. at 1010, the Pilot came aboard and, after slipping the tugs fore and aft, we weighed anchor at 1036. We were at sea in Hervey Bay for the rest of that day and the following day, when 10 Seafires landed on, one bursting a tyre on landing. After some exercises, necessary to keeping 'Arbiter' in tip-top condition and ready for any action that might arise, we returned to harbour. Similar activities continued on the 10th. and the 11th. when the anchor was weighed at 0833. At 1136 a Firefly landed on and another flew off. September 12th. saw a routine day, followed on the 13th. with 'Arbiter' tying up alongside Brettes Wharf to embark aircraft and stores.

10th. September 1945. (Typical Log Record - 12 hours at sea)

0230	Alter course to 265 degrees.
0425	A/c 224 deg.
0600	Call the hands.
0640	A/c 125. Speed 10 knots.
0900	R/U in Hervey Bay.
0904	4 Seafires landed on.
0924	3 Seafires landed on.
0945	3 Seafires landed on.
1044	Commenced Deck landing training.
1155	1 Seafire burst a tyre on landing.
1410	Deck landing training completed.
1445	Special sea dutymen and cable party close up.
1456	Let go starboard anchor. Ship brought up to 6 shackles in 10 fathoms of water.
1515	Fall out Special dutymen.
1740	Sunset.
2100	Rounds.
2235	Pipe down.
	Wind: SE/SW.
	Temperature: 68 degrees.
	Barometer pressure: 1023.
	Miles travelled: 347.
	Number on sick list: 3.
	Zone Time: 10.
	Anchor bearings: Platypus Bay. – Rooney Point 355 degrees.
	– Beacon 132 degrees.

11th. September 1945. At sea, HERVEY BAY. (Typical Log Record)

0600	Call the hands.
0630	Both watches fall in. P.T. on. Flight deck.
0700	Secure.
0800	Hands fall in. Colours.
0810	Special sea dutymen.
0823	Anchor aweigh.
0830	Fall out Special sea dutymen.
0845	Flying stations. Commenced Interception and beacon exercises.
1153	Flying stations secure.
1205	Stop main engines.
1240	R.M.L. alongside. 1 officer landed.
1250	Half ahead 10 knots.
1255	Flying stations.
1536	Landed one Firefly.
1553	Firefly flown off. Lt. Coulson left ship in Firefly for Brisbane.
1631	Let go Port anchor. Ship brought up to 5 shackles in 10 fathoms of water.
1741	Sunset.
2100	Rounds.
2155	Pipe down.

Wind: Mainly E.
Temperature: 68 degrees.
Barometric pressure: 1022.
Miles travelled: 69.
Number on sick list: 4.
Zone Time: 10.
Anchor bearings. Platypus Bay - Rooney Point 353 degrees
- Beacon 073 degrees

Chapter Six

THE HONG KONG EXPERIENCE

We made just two visits to Hong Kong from our Sydney base and both were after the Japanese surrender, the first on 3rd. October 1945, and the second on 3rd. December 1945, a stopping off point during our return trip to England, our Pacific War duty almost completed.

I had no idea what to expect from our first visit to Hong Kong, the extent of my travels prior to joining the Royal Navy had been no further that Southend on Sea! My education, geographically speaking, had done little to prepare me for foreign climes and all that I knew about Hong Kong was that it was a far off place and, when 'made in Hong Kong' was stamped on something I had bought, it meant tawdry and of poor quality. I had read somewhere that 'East and West, never the twain shall meet', and my visit tended to underline that vision. At that time the gulf between the two cultures

Hong Kong from the air.

was a wide one, but now the differences are being steadily ameliorated. The bridge between East and West, as far as I was concerned, had started to take shape as our 'voyage' proceeded, with the visit to Africa and India, i.e. getting used to 'peoples' other than our own, but of course that differences between the Australian culture (similar to our own) and that of Hong Kong were dramatic. I must confess that my feelings were ones of slight apprehension, this step into the unknown. I had visions of dark alleyways, secretive gangs, rickshaws and odd hats etc.! Some of this was true, and we were advised to avoid the dark alleyways. Memories of Hong Kong include seeing endless junks, considerable poverty that contrasted with my one visit to Kowloon by ferry, where I was able to pay a brief visit to a Chinese temple with its mysticism and its magnificence, both outside and inside, beautifully decorated and coupled with an uncanny silence. I do not remember meeting any of the temple personnel.

HONG KONG

An island off the coast of Kwangtung province, China. It lay at the entrance of the Canton River, and was ceded to Great Britain in 1841. Besides the island, which was 11 miles long and from 2 to 5 miles wide the colony included Kowloon, a strip of territory on the mainland, ceded in 1860. To this was added, in 1898, under lease for 99 years, the peninsular south of a line drawn between Deep Bay and Mirs Bay, together with the islands of Lantow and Lamma, the district being known as the Kowloon extension. The concession covered an area of 391 square miles, including the island of Hong Kong, 32 square miles, and had a population of 1,071,893, of whom about 24,125 were non-Chinese.

Kowloon.

Hong Kong – natives selling local produce, fruit etc.

Before 1839 the island of Hong Kong was merely a resort of Chinese fisherman. In that year the English traders came there from Canton. War resulted from an affray on the island in July, during which a Chinese person was killed by some British sailors. The British expedition used Hong Kong as its base and formally took possession of the island in January, 1841, the cession being confirmed by the Treaty of Nanking, 1842; the charter bore the date 5th. April 1843.

The site chosen for the settlement was on the north coast of the island,

A Chinese man.

and the first sale of land took place in June, 1841. The town, called Victoria, stretched 4 miles west to east along a narrow strip of land between the hills and the sea. Hong Kong was, in normal times, the distributing centre for one-fourth to one-third of China's trade. The harbour, of which a magnificent view was obtained from Victoria Peak, a prominent hill used as a residential area commanding the town, was one of the finest in the world, and had ranked fifth in respect of tonnage entered and cleared. Local industries included shipbuilding, rope and cement making, sugar and tin refining and deep-sea fishing.

A Chinese boy.

6th. October 1945. Alongside at Hong Kong. (Typical Log Record)

0615	Call the hands.
0745	Both watches of the hands fall in. Employed part of ship.
0800	Colours. Jeep hoisted out.
1330	Special sea dutymen and cable party close up.
1455	Anchor aweigh.
1545	Ship secured alongside Holt's Wharf, starboard side.
1550	Fall out Special Sea dutymen and cable party.
1630	Clear lower deck. Ship's company addressed by Captain and Surgeon
1700	Starboard watch fall in. Employed on stores.
1908	Sunset.
2100	Rounds.
2155	Pipe down.
	Winds: Light Airs. Temperature: 79 degrees.
	Barometric pressure: 1015.
	Number on sick list: 2.
	1st. part of Port watch on leave from 1700 – 2200.

Hong Kong (7th. October 1945.)

0630 Call the hands.
0800 Colours. Both watches of the hands fall in.
0850 R.C. church party ashore.
0950 Hands to Church.
1030 47 Ratings on passage left ship.
1100 R.C. church party on board.
1910 Sunset.
      Wind: Light Airs/N.
      Temperature: 79 degrees.
      Barometric pressure: 1010.
      Number on sick list: 2.
2100 Rounds correct. Leave to 2nd. part of Starboard watch: 1330 – 2200.
2200 Pipe down.

A SUMMARY OF LIFE ABOARD HMS ARBITER DURING THE MONTH OF OCTOBER 1945.

We were sailing from Leyte (Philippines) to Hong Kong during the 1st. October, entering Hong Kong harbour at 13.30 on October 3rd. where we anchored. Weighing anchor at 0730 on the 4th. we proceeded alongside Holt's Wharf at 15.45, remaining there until 15th. October, during which time normal daily duties were the order of the day, which included employing members of the crew 'storing ship'. Shore Leave, of course, was granted, and a description of Hong Kong is included elsewhere in the book.

On the 15th. October we left Hong Kong in order to return to our main Pacific War base, Sydney, carrying a number of civilians. On the 25th. we exchanged identities with HMS Chaser at 1635, and did likewise with HMS Ruler at 1750, eventually reaching Sydney on the

Alongside at Hong Kong, on the way home. Maquaries Wharf.

26th. October. We had exchanged identities with HMS Termagent earlier in the day. Having anchored for a short time, we weighed anchor at 1310 to proceed to No.14 Pierpoint, where we tied up alongside and disembarked the civilian passengers. Slipping our moorings at 1055 on 29th. October, we moved from Pierpoint to No.2 Berth, Woolloomooloo, staying there until the end of October. We had a Captain Chas. Soper (?) aboard during this period.

A slightly more detailed description of the daily routine followed during our time in Hong Kong Harbour, this can be seen in the two copies of the Log Records (6th. and 7th. October) accompanying this chapter, but it is fair to say that nothing at all dramatic occurred whilst we were there.

One of my memories of HMS Arbiter's time in the Pacific War Zone, a picture quite at odds with the elements connected with war, was the feeling of peace when, as 'Arbiter' sailed alone, cutting through a glassy sea, undisturbed by wind, waves or weather and with a full moon shining out of the cloudless sky, I strolled along the flight deck alone in the dark of the night, the only sound disturbing the uncanny quiet being that of the ship passing through the seamless ocean.

Another experience worth recalling was that of porpoises swimming at speed in front of our bow, no matter what speed we were travelling, leaping out of the water with such elegance and underlining the fact that, whatever mankind invented to sail on the seas, nature had done it better.

An item from South China Morning Post & The Hong Kong Telegraph, December 12, 1945.

RADIO HONG KONG

Classical Request Hour. ZBW Hong Kong broadcasting on a frequency of 640 Kilocycles and from 12.30 to 1.30 p.m., 6.30 to 7.30 p.m. and 9.00 to 11.00 p.m. also on 9.52 Megacycles. H.K.T.

12.30	Daily Programme Summary.
12.32	Nat Gonella and his Georgians.
12.45	"Serenade to the Stars" ENSA.
1.00	News and Announcements.
1.10	Alfredo and his Orchestra.
1.30	Film Selections.
2.00	Close Down.
6.30	Rimsky-Korsakov - "Le Coq D'Or" suite.
7.00	London Relay – News.

7.15	"Donald Peers" ENSA.
7.30	Half an hour of Dance Music.
8.00	Classical Request Hour.
9.00	London Relay – News.
9.05	"Fanfare 2" ENSA.
9.35	Light Orchestral Selections.
10.18	"Aida" – Verdi - Act 1.
11.00	Close Down.

(Programmes marked ENSA are recorded specially for Service Entertainment by the Department of National Service Entertainment.)

Other items from South China Morning Post & The Hong Kong Telegraph, December 12, 1945.

FORCES ENTERTAINED
Prominent Local Chinese Giving Parties.

A scheme has been organised by a number of prominent Chinese residents in Hong Kong to entertain Service personnel by way of a series of daily luncheon parties. These parties, which are held at the Tai Tung Restaurant, started on Monday, and it is hoped that these will be 100 in all. Every day 21 Service guests are entertained, men of the Navy, Army and Royal Air Force being invited in proportion to the numbers of the three Services at present in the Colony.

PREPARED TO USE GAS
Japanese Had Stocks Ready for Invasion Troops.
Applied on Biak Island.

Tokyo, Dec. 10.
The Japanese had stocks of gas for use against the United States invasion troops, Brigadier-General Charles E. Loukes, Chemical Officer on General MacArthur's Staff, revealed today. However, he added that American troops were adequately equipped against it.

In Biak Island on March 5, nauseous gas was used by the Japanese against United States troops, but no deaths were caused. The Japanese stopped production of gas in 1943, when the Allies declared that they would not use gas first.

General Loucks further revealed that tens of thousands of Japanese gas bombs and shells had been dumped by the occupation troops. United Press.

A Hong Kong street.

Hong Kong street traders.

JAPS HAD JET-FIGHTER

Quick Climbing Plane That Was Never Used.

Tokyo, Oct. 23.

When the Pacific war ended the Japanese were manufacturing a rocket-propelled fighter designed to counter the Super-Fortresses. It never went into action. The new fighter, known as Shusui, was claimed by the Japanese aeronautical experts to be capable of a very high altitude and a quick rate of climb. It could fly for seven minutes, but was constructed to glide back to its base. The fighter had a wide fuselage and curving tail. It was equipped with four 3m.m. guns. A special school was set up to train pilots, and special dishes were served the airmen so that they could withstand altitude. The menu consisted mainly of meat, and no starch was allowed.

FURTHER BACKGROUND TO HONG KONG
BEFORE, DURING AND AFTER WW2

Hong Kong, created a crown colony in 1843 was, up to 1941, administered by a governor, assisted by an executive council and a legislative council. Plans were announced in 1946 for revising the constitution, so as to permit a larger measure of self-government.

On December 8th. 1941, following the outbreak of World War II, two Japanese divisions, supported by dive-bombers, launched an attack on the colony from the landward side. The assault was repulsed by the garrison that was comprised of Canadian, British and Indian troops. Strong pressure necessitated the withdrawal of British forces at Kowloon to Hong Kong on the night of December 11th –12th. A demand of surrender was refused, and there followed three days of intense air, naval and artillery bombardment, followed by a second ultimatum, that was also rejected.

On 18th. December, Japanese forces succeeded in crossing the narrow strait separating the island from the mainland and penetrated the defences. Counter-attacks failed, and by 22nd. the defenders were split into isolated groups, lacking air support, supplies, ammunition and water. The reservoirs had fallen into Japanese hands and the water mains had been destroyed by bombardment. Outnumbered five to one, the garrison surrendered on Christmas Day.

The Japanese occupation terminated on 30th. August 1945, when a powerful British naval force entered the harbour. Except for a sharp clash with Japanese 'suicide' troops in the dockyard area, the reoccupation was orderly. Hong Kong had been badly damaged, many public buildings, including the university, being in ruins, while the results of thirty years afforestation had been destroyed. The formal Japanese surrender was made at Government House on 16th. September. After the war, Hong Kong suffered an acute shortage of houses and food, while there was an influx of Chinese seeking refuge from the disturbed mainland. This, I suppose, made it easier for the post-war modernisation of Hong Kong, the modern city, with its mushrooming of sky scrapers, bearing no relation to the Hong Kong that I visited.

The University of Hong Kong, a British University, was founded in 1911. Its nucleus was a college of medicine, and it was opened in 1912, Sir Charles Eliot being the first president. There were faculties of medicine, engineering, science and arts. As mentioned earlier, the buildings were destroyed in the Second World War.

The Japanese of course had left Hong Kong before we visited it the first time, otherwise we could not have berthed there, and amongst the memorabilia that I brought back I found a China Fleet Club bill for 8 dollars 25 cents, the cost of a meal for four of us, and which consisted of 3 lobster salads, egg and chips and 4 cups of tea, about £1.50 at today's rate of exchange – I cannot remember who paid! It would seem that I also visited a Naval tailor, clothier and general outfitter by the

The bill for meals at the China Fleet Club.

A business card from a tailor.

The silk scarf which I still possess.

name of 'Cheong Seng' from Shanghai, where I must have purchased a beautifully embroidered (a dragon motif) silk scarf that, incidentally, I still possess.

Hong Kong is no longer a British Crown Colony and was returned to, and became an integral part of China at the end of June 1997. The island was ceded to Great Britain in the Treaty of Nanking (1842); part of the Kowloon Peninsula was acquired (1860); and the New Territories were leased to Great Britain for 99 years in 1898. In 1984 Britain and China agreed that at the end of 1997 Hong Kong would be returned to China as a Special Administrative Region, with social and economic systems to continue unchanged for 50 years. Hong Kong remains a free port and a major commercial, banking and manufacturing centre.

Chapter Seven

HOME TO 'BLIGHTY'

We started the journey home in November 1945 and detoured via Hong Kong to pick up a number of civilians, including women and children. We had to be very creative to find activities to keep our guests occupied, especially the children, on the month-long journey, mostly at sea. In fact we reached Hong Kong on 3rd. December 1945.

It wasn't until 17th. that we called at Singapore, albeit briefly, presumably to take on supplies and fuel. Then followed the three-day trip to Trincomalee,

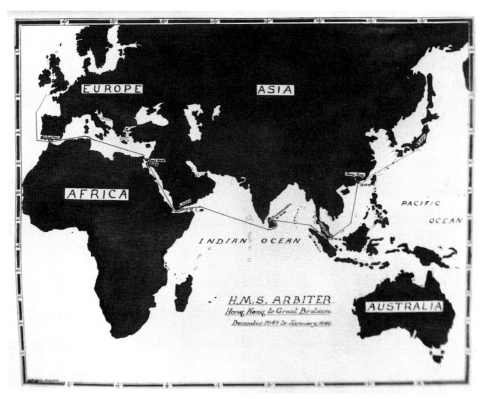

A map showing the route back to 'Blighty'.

Rough Sea! Sailing through the Mediterranean en route to England (Jan. 3rd. 1945).

across the Arabian Sea to Aden, and thence to Port Said at the North end of the Suez Canal, arriving there on New Year's Day. On the outward trip I mentioned the calmness of the Mediterranean Sea and, foolishly, I thought it was usual for this stretch of water. How wrong I was. We learned, rather worryingly, that a ship similar to ours was foundering, due to the very rough sea and, to add to my consternation, whilst I was in the capacious hangar, I could see the hull plates moving against each other, part of the intended construction to avoid impossible strain on the ship's shell. The sea was such that we endured excessive rolling rather than pitching, and at time I wondered whether we would ever regain equilibrium, but 'Arbiter' was a survivor, and we benefited from this. As far as I can remember, this was the most uncomfortable time during our 60,000 mile round trip. I was relieved to reach

Gibraltar on 5th. January 1946, and I was even happier when we reached Lands End on 8th. January 1946.

I spent some months at HMS Drake, Devonport prior to de-mobilisation, and can remember the blue suit with which I was issued, to enable me to reintegrate with civilian life, something that was to prove somewhat difficult after five years of experience in widely varying theatres of war.

One of the things with which I always had a little difficulty during my naval career was being ordered about by incompetent officers etc., some of whom had been plucked out of 'Civvy Street' just like myself and who revelled in their new found power, against whom there was no comeback for us lesser mortals, certainly not in wartime. Having said that, I came into contact with officers and men who I counted as my friends, and my friendship with them would have been the same in civilian life also. I never really got used to being 'cheek by jowl' with my fellow men, with complete lack of privacy, but the discipline required to be an efficient member of the forces has stood me in good stead as a member of the human race.

As I mentioned earlier, I carry happy memories of the kindness of the Australian people.

As some people have observed, the Japanese had been defeated before the Atomic Bombing, with their fleet virtually destroyed and, because of the devastating bombing of the mainland of factories, airports, the creation of shortages of supplies, ammunition, fuel etc., but whether it was because they did not know it, or pride did not allow them to admit defeat, perhaps we will never know. Even had a surrender been agreed, there would have been large numbers of Japanese Commanders who would have fought on to save their honour, and it would have been messy, with continuing loss of life on both sides. Suffice to say, the dropping of the Atomic Bombs saved the lives of considerable numbers of British, American and other allied servicemen.

The Last Word

I shall leave the last word to a James F. Forrest, a columnist for a Far East newspaper, namely the 'South China Morning Post and Hong Kong Telegraph, dated Wednesday, 12th. December 1945.

I used part of his column earlier in the book, but he ends the column with the following words, under the caption:

H.M.S. Arbiter

Sailing for England Tomorrow

Took Repatriates Home

'It was, until recently, the privilege of destroyers to be called the Royal Navy's "maids of all work". Time and circumstances have altered that however, and the descriptions may now also be applied to escort carriers. Such a ship is HMS Arbiter, which is due to sail tomorrow from Hong Kong to the United Kingdom. She will thus bring near completion a record of meritorious service.

During her days with the British Pacific Fleet, HMS Arbiter's crew worked hard days and nights in support of the main fleet by ferrying aircraft, fuel and supplies to the forward areas. The heat was almost overwhelming, but the replenishing, without which the Fleet could not have maintained in action for so long, was continued. During her three and a half months separation from base, the ship's company had to be content with shore-leave on a barren Pacific Island and an occasional swim in the water of Manus harbour.

After the end of the war, she (HMS Arbiter) returned to Sydney, was hastily converted into a "Mercy Ship" and came to Hong Kong to assist in the task of repatriating P.O.W.'s and internees.

Many of the Hong Kong people who travelled by the 'Arbiter' wrote back to their friends here, telling of the kindness of the ship's officers and crew and the unstinted care and attention given to them.

This is, therefore, her second visit to Hong Kong and her work is almost finished. Her future is uncertain. It is probable, however, that with the termination of "Lend-Lease", she will return to the United States for disposal.

On the bridge structure of the ship is a plaque bearing a bronze figure of "Astraea" the "Goddess of Justice" in Greek mythology. Beneath this is printed in gilt letters the ship's motto "Jus a Calls", the meaning of which is "Justice from the Skies", and it is a motto that her present Commanding Officer, Captain C.W. Byas, R.N., and all who have served aboard her may rightly be proud. It is a motto which, if not earned in existing action, has most certainly been justified in monotonous deed.'

I think James Forrest, in the column as a whole, aptly and independently describes HMS Arbiter's role in the Pacific War much better than my words can as an individual closely involved in the conflict, giving, as it were, an onlooker's view of the activities of one of the ships that made up the British Pacific Fleet.

December 1945 – The journey home, based on the Log Book Record.

1st. Sailing from Manus to Hong Kong, calling at Manila Bay.
  1330 Passengers embarked for Hong Kong.
  1516 Anchor Aweigh.
2nd. Manila Bay to Hong Kong.
3rd. At sea – Manila to Hong Kong.
  0945 Arrive Hong Kong. Ship alongside Mackays Wharf.
  Drafts for ships and shore leaving throughout the day.
4th. Hong Kong – ship's duties.
5th. Ditto. One cell offender discharged to Rd. D.Q. Hong Kong under escort.
6th. Ditto. Storing ship.
7th. Ditto. Storing ship.
8th. Ditto. Disinfecting mess deck spaces.
9th. (Sunday). Employed Ship's duties.
  0900 Hands to Divine Service.
  Store ship.
10th. Hong Kong. 0745 Clear lower deck – lay all bedding on flight deck.
11th. Ditto. Employed ship's duties and storing ship.
12th. Ditto Employed ship's duties and storing ship.
  1700 Civilian passengers embarked, also 95 ratings from HMS Ardent and 24 Royal Marines.
13th. Hong Kong to Singapore. 1104 Anchor Aweigh. At sea.
14th. At sea.
15th. At sea.
16th. At sea. 0700 Sighted British Trawler E.L. M.I.R.10.
  1500 Sighted land. 1820 Clocks retarded. 1836 Mankai Island sighted.
17th. Arrived at Singapore – anchored in Berth 19 at four shackles.
  1315 Special Sea Duty men and Cable Party close up.
  1420 Anchor Aweigh. 1443 White obelisk abeam 75c.
18th. At sea.
19th. At sea en route to Trincomalee. 1825 Clocks retarded 50 minutes.

20th. At sea. 1530 Clocks retarded one hour.

21st. Arrived at Trincomalee. 0720 Secured one bridle to No.1 buoy.
   1315 Storing ship. 1610 Slow ahead – leaving harbour.

22nd. At sea – Trincomalee to Port Said.

23rd. At sea. 1830 Clocks retarded one hour.

24th. At sea. 1815 Clocks retarded 30 minutes.

25th. (Christmas Day). At sea. 0930 Divine Service.
   Swiss Minister addressed ship's company.

26th. At sea Clocks put back one hour.

27th. Stopped off at Aden.
   0845 Anchored temporarily in 5 fathoms awaiting Pilot.
   1030 Anchor Aweigh. 1041 Secured to No.1 Buoy – Tug left.
   1245 Stored ship. 1630 Left harbour.

28th./29th. At sea. Aden to Port Said via Suez.

30th. At sea 0730 Divine Service. 2200 Entering harbour at Suez to await Pilot.

31st. 1130 Canal Pilot aboard. Anchor Aweigh – courses and speed as
   required for entering Canal. 1217 Entered Canal. 1407 Entered
   Bitter Lakes. 1550 Re-entered Canal. 2330 Anchored Port Said.
   (And so, home to England, via the Mediterranean, Gibraltar etc.).

Chapter Eight

THE BRITISH PACIFIC FLEET

A record of the names of the ships of the Royal Navy, the Royal Australian, New Zealand and Canadian Navies, with those ships of other Allied Nations which operated as units of the British Pacific Fleet in the war against Japan. (In alphabetical order).

Aase, Maersk, Achilles, Activity, Adamant, Advantage, Aire, Aimwell, Alacrity, Amethyst, Anson, Aorangi, Apollo, **ARBITER**, Artifex, Argonaut, Arndale, Aroha, Ariadne, Arbuus, Assistance, Atheling, Atlas, Avon, A.F.D.'s: 17, 18, 20.

Bacchus, Barle, Ballarat, Bathurst, Barbain, Barfleur, Barthorpe, Belfast, Bendigo, Bermuda, Berryhead, Beachy Head, Begum, Berwick, Bishopsdale, Black Swan, Black Prince, Bonaventure, Bosphorous, Broome, Brown Ranger, B.Y.M.'s: 2064, 2153, Burnie.

Cairns, Cap Des Palmes, Castlemaine, Carella, Cedardale, Cessnock, Ceylon, Cheerly, Chaser, Challenger, City of Dieppe, City of Paris, Clan, Chatton, Colossus, Corinda, Crane.

THE BRITISH PACIFIC FLEET (II)

Darvel, Daarst Creek, Devonshire, Denbighshire,
Deersound, Derg, Destiny, Dingledale,
Duke of York, Dullisk Cove.

Eaglesdale, Edna, Empire Battleaxe, Empire Clyde,
Empire Charmian, Empire Crest, Empire Josephine,
Empire Lagan, Empire Mace, Empire Sam, Empire Silver,
Empire Spearhead, Enchantress, Erne, Euryalus.

Fencer, Fernmoor, Findhorn, Flamborough Head,
Fort Alabama, Fort Constatine, Fort Colville, Fort Dunvegan,
Fort Edmonton, Fort Langley, Fort Kilmar, Fort Providence,
Fort Wrangel, Formidable, Freemantle.

Gambia, Gawler, Geraldton, Gerusalemme, Glenartney,
Glenearn, Glenstrae, Glory, Golden Meadow, Goulburn,
Green Ranger, Grenville, Guardian, Gedrun Maersk, Gurna.

A BPF ship photographed from HMS Arbiter – HMS Resolution.

HMS Newfoundland.

THE BRITISH PACIFIC FLEET (III)

Hart, Helford, Hernelin, Heron, Heros, Hind, Howe, H.D.M.L.'s: 1440, 1449, 1474, 1475, 1483, 1489, 1493.

Idomeneus, Iere, Illustrious, Implacable, Indefatigable, Indomitable, Integrity, Ipswich.

Jaarstrom - Kalgoorlie, Kelantan, Kempenfelt, Kheti, King George V, King Salvor, Kistna, Kola.

Lamont, Lancashire, Lariat, Launceston, Leonian, Lewes, Lismore, Loma, Novia, Lothian.

Marudu, Maryborough, Manxman, Maunganui, Maidstone, Mildura, Montclare, Mull of Galloway, M.F.V.'s: 31, 98, 156, 164, 166, 167, 181, 197, 243, 244, 245, 280, 411, 424, 723, 749, 751, 753, 785, 792, 794, 796, 906, 1017, 1040, 1044, 1046, 1069, 1071, 1089, 1092, 1102, 1103, 1127, 1155, 1156, 2046.

THE BRITISH PACIFIC FLEET (IV)

Napier, Nepal, Newcastle, Newfoundland,
Nizam, Norman.

Odzani, Olna, Ontario, Oxfordshire.

Pachecho, Parrett, Pheasant, Pioneer, Pirie, Plym,
Priam, Prince de Liege, Prince Robert,
Princess Maria, Pia, Prome.

Quadrant, Quality, Queenborough, Quiberon,
Quickmatch, Quilliam.

Rapidol, Reaper, Redpole, Resource, Robert Maersk,
Rockglen, Rockcliffe, Rockwing, Ruler, Rockmount,
Royal Netherlands, Submarines: 0.19, 0.21, 0.23, 0.24.

HMS Swiftsure.

HMS Turbulent.

THE BRITISH PACIFIC FLEET (V)

St. Margaret's, Salvestor, Salvictor, San Adolfo,
San Amado, San Ambrosio, San Andres, Scorcher,
Scotsman, Sea Nymph, Sea Scout, Selene, Serbol,
Seven, Sisters, Sidon, Slesvig, Sleuth, Slinger, Solent,
Southern Prince, Spark, Speaker, Spearhead, Spirit,
Sprightly, Springdale, Spur, Stagpool, Stawell, Sturdy,
Strahan, Sibyl, Striker, Stubborn, Stygian, Suffolk,
Supreme, Swiftsure.

Taciturn, Tamworth, Tantalus, Tapir, Taurus, Teazer,
Telemachus, Tenacious, Termagent, Terpsichore,
Terapin, Thorough, Thule, Thyras, Tiptoe, Titjerhaa,
Tjitja-Lengka, Toowoomba, Totem, Tradewind,
Trenchant, Tromp, Troubridge, Trump, Tudor, Tumult,
Turpin, Tuscan, Tyne, Tyrian, Tugs (Tanac): 113, 114, 117,
135, 153, 155, 156, 172, 173, Tugs (Tusa): 224, 226, 227, 230.

Uganda, Ulysses, Ulster, Undaunted, Undine, Unicorn,
Urania, Urchin, Ursa, Usk.

THE BRITISH PACIFIC FLEET (VI)

Vacport, Vasna, Venerable, Vengeance, Victorious,
Vindex, Virtue, Voracious, Vox.

Wager, Wagga, Wakeful, Wave Governor, Wave Emperor,
Wave King, Wave Monarch, Wave Regent, Weazel, Wessex,
Whelp, Whimbrel, Whirlwind, Whyalla, Wide-Mouthbay,
Wizard, Woodcock, Woolongong, Wrangler.

XE I (Executioner) XE II (Xerces) XE III (Sigyn)
XE IV (Exciter) XE V (Perseus) XE VI (Excaliber II)
Zwaardvisch

THE BRITISH PACIFIC FLEET (VII)

Depot Ships of the Royal Australian Navy placed at the disposal of the British Pacific Fleet on the Australian Station:

Kuttabul, Penguin, Rushcutter, Maitland, Cerebus, Lonsdale, Moreton, Magnetic, Kuranda, Basilisk, Ladava, Madang, Melville, Leeunwin, Torrens, Huon.

Royal Navy Shore Establishments:

Golden Hind I, Woolloomooloo (Sydney), Furneaux, Nabreekie (Monab VII), Napsford (Brisbane), Beaconsfield (Melbourne), Pepys (Manus), Tamar, Nabcatcher (Monab VIII), (Hong Kong); Nabberley (Monab II), (Bankstown); Nabswick (Monab V), (Jervis Bay), Nabstock (Monab VI), (Maryborough); Nabbington (Monab I), (Nowra); Nabaron (Monab IV), (Ponam); Nabthorpe (Monab III), (Schofields).

Royal Marine Establishments:

Port Stephens, Moore Park.

Appendix A

HMS ARBITER'S PACIFIC TRIP
(60,000 MILES)

1st. March 1945.   Left Greenock.
9th. March 1945.   Reached Gibraltar.
19th. March 1945.   Port Said (Africa).
20th. March 1945.   Suez (Africa).
28th. March 1945.   Bombay (India).
1st. April 1945.   Colombo (Ceylon).
4th. April 1945.   Cochin (India).
8th. April 1945.   Trincomalee (Ceylon).

(Non-stop from Trincomalee to Sydney)

Sydney (Australia).

Trips from Sydney to the Fleet off Japan transporting aircraft, spares and supplies, including calling at Hong Kong (3rd. October and 3rd. December 1945) the Philippines (Manus and Leyte) and Brisbane. (2 weeks on a farm in the Blue Mountains).

3rd. December 1945.   Hong Kong.(return trip to England).
17th. December 1945.   Singapore.
21st. December 1945.   Trincomalee.
27th. December 1945.   Aden.
31st. December 1945.   Suez.
1st. January 1946.   Port Said.
5th. January 1945.   Gibraltar.
8th. January 1945.   Blighty – Lands End.

Appendix B

THE FINAL PAGE
(AFTER THE DEFEAT
OF THE JAPANESE)

A publication was produced in Australia at the end of the war, summarising and illustrating much of the activity that took place, and printed on the penultimate page was a message from the Commander-in-Chief, British Pacific Fleet that ended with the following words:

> To all who served in the British Pacific Fleet,
> and to all of you in Australia who did so much
> to help us in our difficult task, I tender my heart-
> felt thanks and wish you the very best of luck in
> the future.
>
> BRUCE FRASER
>
> Commander-in-Chief, British Pacific Fleet.

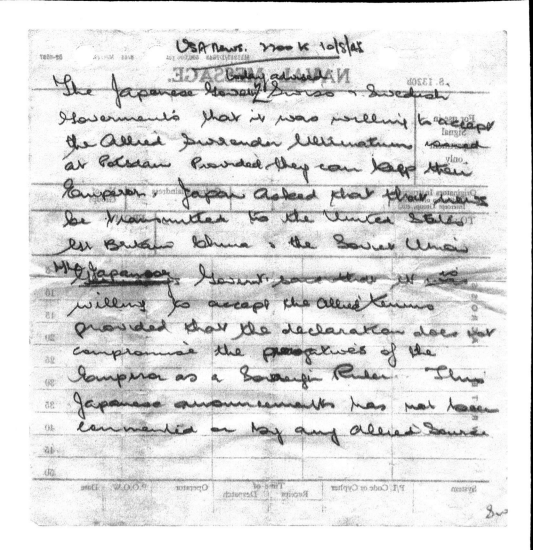

Copy of the Japanese surrender broadcast, written down by Peter Ward at the time.
USA News 2200 K 10/8/45

The Japanese Government today advised the Swiss and Swedish Governments that it was willing to accept the Allied surrender ultimatum issued at Potsdam, provided that they can keep their Emperor. Japan asked that news be transmitted to the United States, Gt. Britain, China and the Soviet Union. The Japanese Government said that it is willing to accept the Allied terms, provided that the declaration does not compromise the prerogatives of the Emperor as Sovereign Ruler. This Japanese announcement has not been commented on by any Allied Source.

Appendix C

THE JAPANESE SURRENDER

It is worth spending a moment filling in the detail of the unconditional Japanese surrender, one of the most significant events in the recent history of the world. The announcement of the surrender was made simultaneously by Mr. Atlee and Mr. Truman to the effect that Emperor Hirohito of Japan would order all his military, naval and air commanders to cease active resistance and surrender their arms.

For Britain, the war had lasted almost six years, and the return to peace was to be celebrated by two days of celebration. There was a broadcast by King George and Mr. Atlee spoke to the nation at midnight by radio, declaring, 'Japan has today surrendered, the last of our enemies to be laid low'.

President Truman addressed the crowds from the portico of the White House saying, 'This is the day we have been waiting for since Pearl Harbour'. USS Missouri was the setting for the brief peace ceremony where the representatives of the Japanese government read a brief statement from Emperor Hirohito, recognising the American victory and acknowledging that US forces under General Douglas MacCarthur would occupy Japan. The general said afterwards, 'It is my earnest hope, and indeed the hope of all mankind, that from this solemn occasion a better world shall emerge out of the blood and carnage of the past'. He went on to say that he was proud of the Allied achievement, but looked forward to a time when both sides would, 'rise to that higher dignity that alone benefits the sacred purposes we are about to serve' It is not generally known that the American Heavy Cruiser, USS Indianapolis's last duty was to carry the atomic bomb to the American base at Guam; she was sunk during enemy action in Philippine waters, with the loss of almost all hands, an example of inverse irony if you like. This sad event, announced by the Navy Department, had an inevitable effect on the celebrations.

It is interesting to note that General MacCarthur received the formal surrender of Japan, bearing in mind his experiences throughout the Pacific War; he had been appointed Supreme Allied Commander on that day. An official Victory Day of celebration was to be announced after the signing of the documents of capitulation. Britain and China would be represented at the ceremony, together with Russia, although the Soviet Union did not declare war on Japan until after the dropping of the atomic bomb. The Russian armies then invaded Japanese Manchuria.

A weeping crowd gathered before the Imperial Palace, wailing and prostrating themselves before the monarch, still worshiped as a god. 'Forgive us, O Emperor', they said, 'We are moved to tears by His Majesty's infinite solicitude'. The transmission then went dead.

It is difficult to recall how one felt at a particular moment in time, especially one sixty years ago, and I am sure that most of those aboard the 'Arbiter' did not realise the magnitude of the event surrounding the dropping of the atomic bombs – we hadn't seen, for example, pictures of the devastation of Hiroshima and Nagasaki – and neither were cognisant of the dramatic effect that the atomic bomb would have in the future. I think that the overall feeling was one of relief, glad to see the end of the Second World War after years of needless slaughter 55,000,000 lives lost, to say nothing of the wounded and maimed) and already coveting thoughts of the return home to become a civilian again, with all the contrast that would be involved and the uncertainty. At least there would be peace!

Appendix D

EPILOGUE

Readers of my first book, 'From Africa to the Arctic' will remember my saying how lucky HMS Beagle was, although the luck was based on good Captaincy and a good crew. My luck as a member of the crew withstood all the might of the German war machine, 'Beagle' surviving Russian Convoys and the 'D' Day Landings etc.

Luck obviously stayed with me on HMS Arbiter, underlined by the fact that I have written book number two, 'Pacific Voyage', although the luck again was based on certain factors such as (1) the Japanese control over large areas of the Far East had diminished greatly, as a result of the determination of the Allied forces, by the time 'Arbiter' arrived on the scene in June 1945 and (2) we never actually entered the area of the Pacific prone to Kamikaze attacks. These were the main hazards, and I cannot remember nature's weather causing us too much concern and discomfort, plus a certain amount of boredom, but these elements are irrelevant in the survival game.

It is, nevertheless, fair comment to say that HMS Arbiter, together with all the other elements of the British Pacific Fleet, played an important part in the quelling of the Japanese war machine, and the survival of the 'Free World'.

Appendix E

RESOURCING MATERIAL
FOR THIS BOOK

The writing of this book has been a very different experience from that of my first book, 'From Africa to the Arctic' (a year on the destroyer HMS Beagle). For the first book, my memory was stimulated by a Diary that I kept (with daily entries), and the Imperial War Museum was able to supply me with some excellent photographs. With this book, there was no Diary, but in its place I had amassed a large number of photographs, many taken by the ship's photographer, of events as they happened. These, together with memorabilia that I had saved, a map that recorded places visited, and newspapers and magazines from Australia etc., were invaluable aids. A visit (with my wife) to the Public Records Office at Kew proved invaluable, monthly 'Log Books' being available, from which we were able to establish day to day detail, thus filling in gaps in my memory. I have also been able to establish contemporary descriptions in words and pictures of places visited during the 60,000 miles round trip, which add 'colour' to the main thrust of the book, the defeat of the Japanese. Sixty years is a long time to recall incidents, activities and feelings etc., but another record of what Peter Smith refers to in his book 'Task Force 57', as the 'forgotten war', of which there are few, cannot be a bad thing.

Many atrocities occurred, perpetrated by the Japanese, that I was fortunate not to have experienced, HMS Arbiter's job being to serve the British Pacific Fleet rather than being part of it, but I have included some facts, figures and descriptions that hint at them. This book is dedicated to those who took part in the 'Pacific War' and were injured, suffered or lost their lives to uphold ideals of decency and freedom, together with those who survived. We thought that the Second World War would make the world a safer place, but recent events make this questionable.

Appendix F

ACKNOWLEDGEMENTS

My thanks to Jean, my wife, for all her help and encouragement throughout the production of this book. My thanks also to daughters Nicky and Sue for their support.

My thanks to friends and relations for their encouragement.

Thanks are also due to the Official Photographer, who served on HMS Arbiter during the time that I was a member of the crew.

Appendix G

BIBLIOGRAPHY

The Public Records Office (Kew, London).
The South China Morning Post & The Hong Kong Telegraph (1945).
Memorabilia and photographs taken at the time (1945).
The Australian magazine 'Pix' published at the time (1945).

Appendix H

ROYAL NAVAL SERVICE SHEET FOR WORLD WAR II – PETER WARD

Shore Establishments	Rating	Period of service & ships served on
Glendower (N. Wales)	Ordinary Seaman	4th. Oct. 1941 - 19th. Nov. 1941
Victory (Isle of Man)	ditto	20th. Nov. 1941 - 18th. Dec. 1941
Victory (HMS Sweet Briar)	ditto	19th. Dec. 1941 - 24th. Apr. 1942
Pembroke	ditto	24th. Apr. 1942 - 25th. Apr. 1942
Badger (Sunk Head Fort)	ditto	25th. Apr. 1942 - 1st. Dec. 1942
Badger (Sunk Head Fort)	ditto	2nd. Dec. 1942 - 14th. Apr. 1943
Mercury	Able Seaman	15th. Apr. 1943 - 16th. Apr. 1943
King Alfred (C.W.Candidate)	ditto	17th. Apr. 1943 - 1st. May 1943
Mercury	ditto	2nd. May 1943 - 10th. May 1943
Drake IV (RDF)	ditto	11th. May 1943- 2nd. June 1943
Orlando (HMS Beagle)	ditto	3rd. June 1943 - 17th. July 1943
Philoctetes (HMS Beagle)	A/Leading Seaman (Radar-Ty)	confirmed 9th. June 1943
Philoctetes (HMS Beagle)	ditto	18th. July 1943 - 13th. Oct. 1943
Orlando (HMS Beagle)	ditto	14th. Oct. 1943 - 29th. Feb. 1944
Orlando (HMS Beagle)	R.P. (P)	1st. Mar. 1944 - 3rd. May 1944
Orlando (HMS Beagle)	A/Leading Seaman (Radar) (Confirmed Leading Seaman (Ty) R.P.2 - 9th. June 1944)	4th. May 1944 - 30th. July 1944
Drake	ditto	31st. July 1944 - 15th. Sept. 1944
Heron	ditto	16th. Sept. 1944 - 27th. Oct. 1944
Valkyrie	ditto	28th. Oct. 1944 - 10th. Nov. 1944
Drake	ditto	17th. Nov. 1944 - 5th. Dec. 1944
HMS Arbiter	ditto	6th. Dec. 1944 - 24th. Jan. 1946
Drake	ditto	25th. Jan. 1946 - 25th. May 1946

Appendix I

PETER WARD – BACKGROUND

Peter Ward is the author of this book, 'A Pacific Voyage'. The book is based on his experiences as a crew member of HMS Arbiter, an Escort Carrier based in Sydney, Australia and a unit of the British Pacific Fleet during the year 1945, the Fleet being an important element in the defeat of the Japanese.

His first book, 'From Africa to the Arctic', was published in April 2003. Based on a Diary, it recalled his life aboard the destroyer, HMS Beagle during the Year June1943 to June 1944, that was involved in Russian Convoys and the 'D' Day Landings.

Peter was born in 1922. Both his parents were musical and he was educated at Walpole Grammar School, Ealing, London, during which time he learned to play the piano and violin. He has always been involved in the world of 'Classical Music'. After a period of working for the Inland Revenue, he joined the Royal Navy in September 1941, qualifying as a Radar operator in Douglas, Isle of Man. From there he joined the Corvette, 'HMS Sweet Briar', only to find himself based in Iceland and involved in patrolling the North Atlantic Ice Barrier in search of a German Battleship.

Fortunately for him no contact was made! Following a year on a Fort off the East Coast on Sunk Head Sands, he joined the crew of HMS Beagle, a destroyer, for the period of one year.

The last year of the Second World War saw Peter as a crew member of HMS Arbiter, the reason for the writing of this present book, helping to serve the British Pacific Fleet off the coast of Japan, during which time VE and VJ days were celebrated.

After the war, Peter trained as a teacher at University College, Worcester, and from there he went on to study at the Birmingham School of Music, now Birmingham Conservatoire, where he studied both piano and violin. He took up a teaching post as music specialist in Oxford, followed by a Deputy Headship, concluding his teaching career as a Senior Lecturer in Music at Summerfield College, Kidderminster and Shenstone/N.E.W. College Bromsgrove. Having already obtained three LRAM Diplomas in the early 1950's, he gained an Open University BA Honours Degree in the 1980's.

In 1980 he was jointly responsible, with Louis Carus the then Principal of the Birmingham School of Music, what is now the Birmingham Conservatoire Association, a support group made up from Lecturers, Friends, Alumni etc., of the Conservatoire. He was awarded an Honorary Fellowship by Birmingham Conservatoire in 1996 for services to music. With Joyce Messenger, he initiated and helped to organise the Bromsgrove Festival Young Musicians' Platform for twelve years, and was pianist for Barnt Green Choral Society, also for twelve years. He has been Staff Tutor for the Orchestral Courses at Hawkwood College, Stroud for over thirty years, as well as performing, teaching, adjudicating and serving on numerous committees Peter has been married to Jean for over fifty years, and they have two daughters, Nicola and Susan, both professional musicians. He has appreciated her help and encouragement throughout the production of this book.

Appendix J

SIXTY YEARS ON –
HEROES OF THE ARCTIC CONVOYS

VISIT TO RUSSIA: 4th – 12th MAY 2005
During the year 2005 many veterans of World War II are being encouraged to revisit the theatres of war in which they participated. This has been made possible by the financial support from the National Lottery Hero's Return Scheme.

A large number of British veterans, with their wives, carers etc., that included my wife and myself, left Heathrow on the morning of 4th May to fly to Moscow

Jean and Peter Ward at the British Embassy, Moscow, with the Kremlin in the background, across the river, 5th May 2005.

Peter Ward, marching with other British veterans towards the centre square in Murmansk for the ceremony on 9th May, 2005, the 60th anniversary of the end of the European part of World War II.

for the start of our visit to Russia, to include the celebration of the 60th. anniversary of the 'Patriotic War' victory, as the Russians refer to it. The group was largely made up from members of the North Russia Club and the Russian Convoy Club.

A full programme had been organised, and choices of venues to visit whilst in Murmansk were confirmed at a meeting in the British Embassy in Moscow on the morning of the 5th May. We had virtually two days to explore Moscow before flying to Murmansk. My wife and I were able to explore a part of the Kremlin and I was able to lay a carnation on the grave of the unknown warrior.

We flew to Murmansk on 6th May, the start of a very enjoyable stay at the Polyarnie Zori Hotel, from where our visits were to start. We were treated like royalty in Murmansk, with police escorts for our convoys of coaches to Aloysha, the Grave of the Unknown Warrior, the Northern Fleet Museum, an excellent school of 8 to 17 year olds (Gymnasium 9) and an impressive service at the Russian Cemetery Extension where the Duke of York read a lesson and wreaths were laid on the graves of British seaman who had lost their lives during Russian Convoy duty in the 1940's.

The Russian Cemetery Extension where many British Seamen are buried.

The demeanour of those present showed the strong emotions that were still alive and were embodied in this memorable occasion. Members of the crew of HMS Sutherland formed a guard of honour.

The main celebration took place on 9th May, a day after the Moscow event, with a military parade in the Square, in which the marching veterans took their place, receiving the cheers of the Russians lining the streets. The Duke of York made a speech and, at the close of the ceremony, mixed with the veterans, shaking hands with many of us.

We were frequently 'toasted' during our visit, not least at the reception given for by the Governor of Murmansk us in a crowded room of the Arktika Hotel, another of the hotels at which the veterans were staying, and at which the tables were laden with exotic food and an abundance of drinks, including vodka! We were also given presents of books, vodka etc., beautifully packaged for the occasion.

HMS Sutherland, a nine- year old British frigate berthed in Murmansk dockyard for the celebrations, and veterans were entertained at cocktail parties thrown by the Captain and given guided tours. It would seem that the whole of the Murmansk populous gathered at each of the celebrations, showing their lasting gratitude for the Allies invaluable help during World War II; it involved the delivery of four million tons of war equipment to Russia between 1941 and 1945.

Our Murmansk visit was much enhanced by the company of group of attractive, English-speaking, Russian University students (there was one male) who stayed with us throughout our visit, acting as interpreters and helpers.

Grateful thanks are due to Peter Skinner and Gordon Long, together with the British Embassies in Moscow and St. Petersburg and the officials in Murmansk for their years of work to ensure the success of the 60th. VE anniversary celebrations.

Peter Ward – May 2005 (ex HMS Beagle)